Coaching for Growth

Strategies for exponential growth, empowerment of your team, and for eliminating poor performance.

Paul Hylenski

ISBN: 978-1-0878-9053-1

DEDICATION

Growth is intentional. This book is dedicated to all of the leaders and work families that have helped me to always keep growing. Together we are redefining leadership and changing the world.

CONTENTS

FOREWORD

In preparation to write this book (my second) I wanted to pick a topic that went synchronously with my vision of changing the world through a more human-centered leadership style. Coaching employees is at the very heart of that. Coaching can look like many things. It can be mentoring, daily check-ins, or periodic touchpoints, and it can come in both negative and positive tones. Coaching is critical to developing trust and an open relationship with your teams.

Leadership is much like parenting in many fashions but is not treated that way in the business world. We treat people in our teams, especially poor performers like they are unwanted and sometimes cast them out. While there are times, unfortunately, that are necessary this should be a last resort. Only after every attempt to coach and improve is done, can the final step be taken. When children make mistakes or poor decisions, we do not immediately cast them out of the house. We persuade them with conversations and lessons about what they did, and if needed, then we discipline them. Most of the time, the first mistakes are not met with banishment. There is progressive discipline much like a business environment. The sole purpose of discipline is to change behavior. It should be used as such.

Good mentors and coaches can change the entire experience at work. They can even drastically enhance a person's home life. Throughout life and especially at work, lessons are learned, and mistakes are made. If we can come together, especially as leaders, and focus on a strategic path to coach our teams, the environments will change. This will change our people and give them the feedback they need and, most likely, are yearning for.

I have had great mentors and I have had poor leaders. There is a distinct difference. I am so grateful each day for the teams that I have had the pleasure and honor to work with and lead and I am humbled by the leaders whom I have had the honor of serving under. These leaders shaped me and by utilizing this method we have reshaped business and our teams. The strategy in this book is real-life enacted. This works and is still being used to transform businesses. It may take a different shape or be slightly different depending on your organization, but the overall strategy works and develops an environment of psychological safety and a growth mindset for our teams. That, in my opinion, is the true job of a servant leader. Grow your teams, make their lives better each day, and change their life trajectory every chance you have.

1 THE HUMAN NEED FOR COACHING

In today's competitive workplace, organizations must find innovative ways to maintain a talented and engaged workforce. As the landscape of the workplace evolves, so do the strategies for retaining and developing employees. One of the most effective strategies to emerge is the use of coaching and mentoring within the workplace.

Coaching and mentoring are often used interchangeably, but they are distinct practices with different approaches. Coaching is a structured relationship, typically between a manager or senior-level professional and a younger employee. In this relationship, the coach acts as a facilitator of learning and development. The coach helps the employees identify their own goals and develop the skills necessary to achieve them.

Mentoring, on the other hand, involves a more long-term relationship between a more experienced and knowledgeable mentor and a mentee. In this relationship, the mentor provides guidance and advice to the mentee, usually based on the mentor's own experiences. The mentor is a role model, helping the mentee to gain perspective and grow in their field.

The benefits of coaching and mentoring in the workplace are plentiful and profound. Studies have shown that organizations that invest in coaching and mentoring are more likely to retain their talent and experience more successful employee performance. Coaching and mentoring can help employees develop valuable skills such as problem-solving, leadership, and communication. As employees are better able to manage their career development, they can create growth opportunities for themselves and their organizations.

Not only do these practices benefit the individual, but they also benefit the organization. Studies show that organizations that invest in coaching and mentoring programs have a higher employee retention rate, which leads to decreased costs associated with hiring and training new employees. Coaching and mentoring can also help promote a culture of collaboration and innovation, which can lead to greater success and productivity.

Organizations must realize the importance of developing their employees to remain competitive. Coaching and mentoring are effective tools to help employees reach their goals and improve performance. When done right, these practices can be a great way to engage and motivate employees, build trust, and create a culture of growth and development.

The benefits of coaching and mentoring are real and measurable. Organizations must invest in these practices if they are to remain competitive in the ever-changing world of the workplace. Coaching and mentoring can help employees reach their individual goals and help organizations achieve their overall objectives. By investing in the development of their employees, organizations can create an engaged and productive workforce that is ready to take on the challenges of the future.

Coaching employees is a critical element to successful business management and corporate culture. It is through coaching that leaders develop the skills of their employees, allowing them to perform at their highest level and achieve success. A leader who can effectively coach employees can create an environment that encourages learning, growth, and innovation. One of the most successful examples of a leader who could effectively coach employees was legendary football coach Vince Lombardi. His approach to coaching employees was one of tough love, with an emphasis on developing a powerful team spirit and a dedication to excellence.

Vince Lombardi was born on June 11, 1913, in Brooklyn, New York. He grew up in a strict Roman Catholic family and was coached by his father at a young age. Lombardi was small as a child and was often overlooked while playing football which made him determined to be the best. He attended Fordham University and then served in World War II in the U.S. Army. After the war, he took a job as the offensive coordinator for the New York Giants and eventually became the head coach in 1954.

Vince Lombardi was a leader who believed

that "winning isn't everything, it's the only thing." He was renowned for his motivational techniques, which focused on building a winning team. Lombardi was known for having high expectations for his players, and he expected them to strive for perfection in all aspects of the game. However, Lombardi was also known for his love of the game and his respect for his players. Lombardi treated his players like family and was known to offer words of encouragement and support when they were struggling on the field. Despite the high pressure of his coaching style, Lombardi was also known for his deep caring for his players and for his desire to help them reach their potential.

Lombardi's coaching style was based on many of the same principles that are used today in coaching employees. He focused on developing a strong culture of trust and respect, where players felt comfortable speaking with him and sharing their feelings. Lombardi also made sure to build a sense of camaraderie among his players, emphasizing the importance of teamwork and collaboration. From Lombardi's perspective, if a team was to be successful, each player had to contribute and be willing to put their individual goals aside in favor of the team's success.

Lombardi also believed in constant feedback and communication. He expected his players to be open and honest about their performance, and he was always available for one-on-one conversations to discuss both their successes and failures. Lombardi believed that creating an environment of trust, honesty, and respect was essential for a successful team, and he did what he could to foster this environment. He also made sure to recognize and reward good performances, which motivated his players to keep striving for excellence.

Vince Lombardi's approach to coaching was unique in that it was both tough and caring. He had high expectations for his players and insisted upon excellence, but he also wanted his players to feel supported and valued. Lombardi knew that to be successful, his players needed to be able to trust him and feel like they were part of something bigger. By creating a culture of trust and respect, Lombardi was able to foster an environment where his players could reach their full potential.

Lombardi was also known for his ability to motivate his players. He was able to get the best out of his players and make them believe they could accomplish anything. Lombardi was also an expert strategist and was able to make the right decisions in game-changing situations. He was constantly innovating and evolving his approach to the game and this is why he was so successful.

In today's workplace, successful leaders must also learn how to effectively coach their employees. Just as Lombardi did, they must develop a culture of trust, respect, and collaboration. They must also provide constant feedback, both positive and negative, and they should recognize and reward good performance. Leaders should strive to make their employees feel valued and appreciated, and they should be open and honest in their conversations with them.

Leaders who strive to create an environment of trust and respect, and who are willing to coach their employees to make them better, are leaders who truly care for their employees. Vince Lombardi was a great example of this type of leader, and his success on the football field is a testament to his ability to effectively coach his players to reach their full potential. Leaders who can foster a culture of trust and respect, and who are willing to take the time to coach their employees, will create an environment of success and growth in the workplace.

2 VISION AND PURPOSE CONQUER ALL

Vision and purpose have the power to move mountains, create miracles, and ignite change in the world. It is the driving force that can move a person from a place of obscurity and mediocrity to one of greatness and leadership. In today's world, it is not enough to just have a vision. A leader must have a purpose-driven vision that is inspiring and that stands out from the crowd. A vision and purpose that can make the world a better place.

Samuel Pierpont Langley was an American astronomer, physicist, inventor, and aviation pioneer. He was born in Roxbury, Massachusetts in 1834, and grew up during an age when scientific knowledge and exploration were rapidly increasing. He learned much of his math and physics skills from a local teacher named Joseph

Jenks who lived near the library. His family moved to Detroit in 1847 where his mother died two years later. After her death, he helped raise his younger siblings while attending high school and working as a part-time tutor at the Bird's Aviation School.

Langley was an avid student of mathematics and physics and earned an undergraduate degree from Harvard University in 1859. He taught at the college level in cities across the country before applying for a Navy contract to research flight. Over the next decade, he built several versions of flying machines that were extremely successful in accomplishing short flights, but none had the power to fly over longer distances or on their own. In 1895 he partnered with investors, including Octave Chanute, who was responsible for assembling the most comprehensive collection of human flight data available up to that time. They founded The

Aerial Experiment Association (AEA) which helped promote a special commission to study all existing aeronautical technology. In 1898 he began manufacturing parts for a larger version of his machine and successfully flew it four times on December 17th possibly becoming the first person to fly a heavier-than-air vehicle over a distance greater than 50 feet and powered only by its own propulsion system.

The life and work of Samuel Pierpont Langley is a fascinating example of the sometimes very different paths that visionary individuals can take. Throughout his career, he struggled with balancing ambition with practicality.

Throughout his career, Langley was driven by his ambition to be famous. He coveted and strove for the recognition that came with scientific success. His ambition was so strong that it sometimes overshadowed his scientific research, leading him to pursue projects that seemed more likely to gain public attention, rather than those that were more likely to lead to scientific breakthroughs.

Langley was also driven by a desire for financial success. He wanted to use his scientific skills to make money, and to this end, he pursued projects that could potentially yield large profits. For example, in 1892, he began to develop a revolutionary new type of steam engine, which, if successful, could have brought in a sizable fortune.

In the years leading up to the turn of the twentieth century, Langley devoted much of his time to the study of aeronautics. He was convinced that powered, the heavier-than-air flight was possible, and he wanted to be the first to accomplish it. As a result, he threw himself into the study of flight mechanics and the design of aircraft.

But Langley's approach to designing aircraft was fundamentally different from that of the Wright brothers. The Wright brothers had a vision of improving the lives of people around the world by making air travel a practical reality. They saw their work as a way of changing the world. Langley, on the other hand, saw flight as a way of gaining fame and fortune. He was more interested in the potential rewards of being the first to achieve powered flight than in its wider implications.

The Wright brothers and Langley had fundamentally different approaches when it came to aircraft design. While Professor Langley was very adept at designing technically sound airplanes, the Wright brothers focused their efforts on experimentation and testing. This ultimately led to the downfall of Langley's designs as they could only attain limited success in terms of flight duration and control. On the other hand, the Wright Brothers were able to build an aircraft that successfully flew a sustained, controlled flight for 59 seconds over a distance of 852 feet. Ultimately, Langley's ambition and drive for financial success led to his downfall. While the Wright brothers' vision and dedication enabled them to achieve their goal, Langley's ambition and desire for fame and fortune caused him to take shortcuts and focus too much on the potential rewards of flight. As a result, he was never able to achieve his life's ambition of being the first to fly.

The life and work of Samuel Pierpont Langley provides an interesting case study of the different paths that visionary individuals can take. While Langley was undoubtedly ambitious, his ambition was ultimately his undoing. The Wright brothers, on the other hand, had a clear vision of transforming the world through the power of flight and applied themselves diligently to the task at hand. It was this focus that ultimately enabled them to achieve their goal and revolutionize the world.

The path to a brighter future starts with a vision and purpose. Without a vision, a leader may find themselves at a standstill. They may not know where to go, what to do, or how to get there. Having a clearly defined vision and purpose provides direction, clarity, and purpose. It gives a leader the focus and motivation they need to drive their team forward.

A vision and purpose-driven leader has a strong sense of self-awareness and self-confidence, and they are not afraid to take risks and make difficult decisions. They are passionate about what they believe in and are willing to put in the hard work and effort needed to make their vision and purpose a reality. They have a clear vision of what they want to achieve and the determination to make it happen.

The Wright Brothers is a great example of the power of vision and purpose. Orville and Wilbur Wright were two bicycle mechanics from Dayton, Ohio, who had the vision to build a working airplane. They worked tirelessly for four years and persevered through countless failures and challenges. Despite the opposition and skepticism that they faced, the Wright Brothers had faith in their vision and ultimately created the first successful flying machine.

The visionary leaders of today are no different. They are the ones challenging the status quo, pushing the boundaries of what is possible, and leading the way toward a brighter future. They have a clear vision and purpose, and they are willing to take risks and push themselves and their teams to think differently and innovate.

These leaders are not afraid to face failure and criticism, and they understand the importance of "failing forward". They are not satisfied with the status quo and are constantly striving to create something better, something different. They are not afraid to challenge the traditional way of doing things and to think outside the box. They understand that the only way to make a lasting change is to press beyond the boundaries of what is comfortable and accepted.

A successful leader does not just have a vision and purpose. They also have a strong sense of empathy and an understanding of the needs of others. They are able to listen and connect with their team, understand their challenges and difficulties, and provide the necessary support and guidance needed to help them grow and develop.

Leaders are also able to bring people together and foster collaboration. They recognize that talent is not enough. They foster an environment where people are encouraged to collaborate, innovate, and grow. They understand the importance of having a diverse team and recognize the power of collective ideas.

Leaders are not born, they are made. It takes hard work, dedication, and commitment to make a vision and purpose-driven leader. It takes courage and resilience to push through the fear and the uncertainty. It takes the willingness to try and make mistakes and to learn from them. But more than anything, it takes a vision and purpose to make the world a better place.

The world is full of challenges, and if we want to create lasting change, we need visionary leaders who can lead the way. Leaders who have a clear vision and purpose and are willing to take risks and make hard decisions. Leaders who are not afraid to face failure and criticism and who persevere through it all. Leaders who can inspire, motivate, and drive progress. Leaders who can create a brighter future for us all.

3 GROWTH AND COACHING AREN'T JUST FOR BUSINESS

The United States Marine Corps has been known for decades as an elite force of warriors that have defended America's freedom and interests across the globe. As a result of this, the Marine Corps has become a symbol of strength and discipline, and it takes a special kind of person to be a part of this force. To ensure that the Marines are always performing at their highest level, the Marine Corps has developed a system of providing coaching and feedback to its personnel through Pro and Con evaluations and yearly evaluations for senior ranks.

The Pro and Con evaluations are an efficient and effective way of assessing a Marine's performance and providing constructive feedback. This system consists of two Marines, designated as Pros and Cons, who observe and rate a Marine's performance in a given task or situation. The Pros must find and highlight the positive aspects of the performance, and the Cons must find and emphasize the areas that need improvement. Each Marine is given a score out of 10 for each of the elements being evaluated, and all of the scores are combined to provide a total score. This system provides a systematic method for Marines to receive feedback on their performance and allows them to make improvements and become better Marines.

In addition to Pro and Con evaluations, the Marine Corps also utilizes a yearly evaluation system for senior ranks. This is an intensive and comprehensive assessment of a Marine's performance over the course of the year. Each Marine is evaluated in several different categories, including leadership, physical fitness, combat readiness, and technical proficiency. The overall score is based on a combination of these categories, and each Marine's performance is compared to that of their peers. This evaluation system is essential in ensuring that the Marine Corps continues to maintain a high standard of excellence among its personnel, and it allows upper-level Marines to receive feedback on their performance and strive to improve in areas where necessary.

Performance evaluations and feedback provided by the Marine Corps are essential in helping Marines reach their full potential. The Marine Corps also uses promotion scores as a way to ensure that its best-performing personnel are always growing and developing. Promotion scores are based on a variety of factors, including performance evaluations, technical proficiency, and leadership potential. By using these factors as part of the promotion process, the Marine Corps is able to promote its best-performing Marines, ensuring that top talent is being rewarded and that the Marine Corps remains an elite force.

The Marine Corps culture emphasizes growth and development, and the Marine Corps provides its personnel with resources and support to help them reach their full potential. The Marine Corps offers a variety of professional development courses designed to help Marines develop their leadership and technical skills. The Marine Corps also encourages Marines to pursue additional education and training opportunities to remain competitive and stay ahead of the curve. In addition, the Marine Corps also promotes a culture of self-improvement and encourages Marines to set and pursue personal goals that will help them grow and develop as individuals and as leaders.

The Marine Corps provides a unique and

challenging environment for Marines to grow and develop, and the feedback and evaluation systems provided by the Corps are essential in helping Marines reach their highest potential. By utilizing Pro and Con evaluations and yearly evaluations for upper-level ranks, the Marine Corps can provide its personnel with valuable insight into their performance and provide them with the feedback and guidance necessary to become the best Marines they can be. This feedback and evaluation system ensures that the Marine Corps remains an elite force and that its best-performing personnel is always growing and developing.

My experience in the Marine Corps has been invaluable in my business career. I have been able to apply the skills I have learned in the Marine Corps to my professional life. I have been able to develop my leadership, communication, and coaching skills to be an effective leader in the business world. Being able to lead, motivate, and inspire others has been instrumental in my success. Additionally, I have been able to use my experience in the Marine Corps to stay resilient and adapt to changing situations.

Leadership is a key component of success in any organization. As a Marine Corps Non-Commissioned Officer, I was charged with leading and mentoring my subordinates. I had to learn to effectively make decisions and take responsibility for the outcome. I had to be conscious of how my decisions would affect the overall mission and the morale of my unit. I also had to be able to think on my feet and adapt to changing situations.

Being a leader in the Marine Corps also taught me the importance of communication. As a leader, it was my job to make sure everyone was on the same page. I had to make sure everyone was clear on the mission and their individual roles. I had to be able to effectively relay information to my unit and make sure everyone was on the same page. Additionally, I had to be able to effectively give feedback to my subordinates to ensure their success.

Coaching is also a critical skill I developed during my time in the Marine Corps. As a Marine, I had to coach my unit in order to ensure their success. I had to be able to recognize individual strengths and weaknesses and provide them with the necessary resources and guidance to succeed. I had to be able to motivate and inspire others with my words and actions. Additionally, I had to be able to give effective feedback and provide constructive criticism.

Through my coaching, I was able to identify and correct behaviors and attitudes that were not conducive to mission success. I was able to instill a sense of pride and ownership in my unit and create a culture of excellence. I was also able to help my unit members identify their individual strengths and weaknesses and then coach them on how to use their strengths to improve their performance.

My experience in the Marine Corps has also taught me the importance of resilience and adapting to changing situations. During my time in the Marine Corps, I was continually challenged by new and unexpected scenarios. I had to be able to quickly adapt to changing environments and adjust my strategy accordingly. I also had to be able to stay focused and motivated when things didn't go according to plan. This training, experience, coaching successes and failures, and the need to coach the whole individual prepared me for better coaching in the business environment. Most people think of the Marine Corps and would not envision coaching and evaluations on a granular detail about performance. This is where the Marine Corps and military prepare leaders for a lifetime of feedback giving and taking.

Piloting an aircraft is a complex and demanding job. To ensure the safety of passengers and crew, pilots must maintain a certain level of proficiency and knowledge. Pilots must have comprehensive training and experience in order to be qualified to fly aircraft and fly safely. This training and experience must be updated and maintained on a regular basis.

Training for pilots is a continuous process that involves both formal and informal instruction. Formal training includes courses and programs, such as those provided by the Federal Aviation Administration (FAA). These courses are designed to help pilots obtain and maintain the necessary knowledge and skills to safely fly aircraft. Informal training includes practice and self-study, such as flying solo and attending aviation conferences.

Before a pilot can operate an aircraft, they must first obtain a license. The process for obtaining a pilot's license varies depending on the type of aircraft and the country or region in which the pilot will fly. In the United States, the FAA regulates all aviation activities and issues various certificates and ratings, including the Private Pilot Certificate and the Airline Transport Pilot Certificate. In order to obtain these certificates, pilots must pass a written knowledge test, an oral exam, and a practical flight test.

Additionally, the FAA requires pilots to hold a current medical certificate.
Once a pilot has obtained their license and begun flying, they must undergo periodic reviews with a flight instructor. These reviews help ensure that the pilot is maintaining the required levels of

proficiency and safety. The instructor will evaluate the pilot's performance and make recommendations for improvement. They may also offer additional training if they feel it is necessary.

In addition to reviews with flight instructors, pilots may also be required to attend interviews. During an interview, the pilot is questioned about their safety record and other aspects of their performance. This helps to ensure that the pilot is meeting the necessary standards and is taking the appropriate steps to improve their skills.

The FAA also has programs designed to help pilots stay current and maintain their proficiency. These include recurrent training and proficiency checks (RTPs). RTPs are mandatory for pilots operating commercial aircraft and are designed to ensure that the pilot is up to date on the latest rules and regulations, as well as any changes to aircraft systems. Additionally, RTPs help to assess a pilot's ability to safely operate an aircraft.

In addition to RTPs, many airlines offer specialized training for their pilots. This training is designed to ensure that pilots have the necessary skills and experience to safely fly the airline's aircraft. The training often includes simulator exercises and briefings on operational topics, such as navigation and weather.

In order to help pilots stay safe, many airlines also require their pilots to undergo regular medical examinations. During these examinations, the pilot is evaluated for any medical issues that may affect their ability to fly safely. Additionally, these exams help to ensure that the pilot is fit enough to fly an aircraft.

Pilots must also undergo constant coaching and training to make them better.

Coaching can include one-on-one instruction, feedback on performance, and guidance on how to best utilize the aircraft's systems and equipment. Additionally, pilots may attend conferences or workshops to gain additional knowledge and skills.

Piloting an aircraft is a challenging and demanding job. To ensure the safety of passengers and crew, pilots must have comprehensive training and experience and must update and maintain their proficiency on a regular basis. The FAA has programs designed to help pilots obtain and maintain their licenses and to stay current on the latest rules and regulations. Additionally, many airlines offer specialized training and regular medical examinations to help their pilots stay safe and proficient. Pilots must also undergo constant coaching and training to make them better. By undergoing these programs and training, pilots can ensure that their aircraft and passengers are kept safe.

4 LEADERSHIP BUILDS MOMENTUM

Leadership is a complex endeavor that requires a wide range of skills, from the visionary to the operational. It is not realistic to expect leaders to be perfect, or even close. Leaders, like all of us, are prone to making mistakes. What makes a great leader, however, is their willingness to learn from those mistakes and create an atmosphere of growth and innovation.

The idea that mistakes and failures are unacceptable and oftentimes are met with harsh punishment in business and manufacturing is not conducive to a growth mindset and can create a toxic environment where people are discouraged from taking risks and learning from their mistakes. This kind of attitude can lead to stagnation and lack of innovation, as employees come to fear failure and its repercussions.

The truth is that mistakes are inevitable, and it is important to encourage employees to make mistakes and learn from them. It is through trial and error that we can grow and develop solutions to the problems we face in our work and our lives Without mistakes, there can be no progress.

In business, it is important to create a culture where mistakes are seen as an opportunity to learn. This can be done in a variety of ways, such as providing employees with regular feedback and guidance, creating an open and honest dialogue about mistakes and their repercussions, and providing employees with the tools and resources they need in order to develop the skills and knowledge required to succeed.

It is also important to create an environment where employees feel safe to make mistakes. This includes creating a culture of trust and respect and providing employees with the tools and resources they need to learn from their mistakes. It is also important to ensure that employees feel supported and valued, regardless of their mistakes.

Furthermore, it is important to recognize the value of mistakes and to reward employees for their efforts in learning from them. This could include providing employees with additional training or development opportunities or offering additional compensation or recognition for hard work and perseverance.

It is important to make sure that mistakes are seen as a valuable part of the process of experimentation and innovation. It is through mistakes that new ideas and solutions are discovered and refined. Creative thinking and problem-solving are essential components of success in any business, and mistakes can provide invaluable insight into how to improve processes and products.

In the modern business world, it is no longer acceptable to overlook mistakes or blame employees for them. Instead, it is important to recognize that mistakes are inevitable and to foster a culture of learning and growth. By creating an open and supportive environment where employees feel safe to take risks and make mistakes, organizations can ensure that their employees are productive and motivated and can benefit from the invaluable insights that can be gleaned from making mistakes.

The Growth Environment is a model of leadership that encourages learning from mistakes, rewards creativity, and celebrates the successes of all team members. It emphasizes the importance of open communication, trust, and respect, and nurtures collaboration, innovation, and problem-solving.

At the core of the Growth Environment is the idea that for an organization to succeed, its members must be open to learning from their mistakes, understanding that failure is an inevitable part of growth. Leaders must be willing to admit their mistakes and create an atmosphere where mistakes are not only accepted but also celebrated. This type of open dialogue and learning environment allows for honest feedback and constructive criticism.

A leader in the Growth Environment needs to set an example. They should be open-minded and willing to learn from their own and others' mistakes. They should be able to recognize and reward the effort and progress of those around them. Leaders should also be able to provide clear direction and vision and create a culture that encourages creativity and growth.

Leaders can foster a Growth Environment by creating a culture of trust and respect. This means that they must be willing to listen to their team members, understand their concerns, and value their ideas. Leaders should be open to feedback, provide clear and direct communication, and encourage collaboration. It is also important to recognize the successes of individuals and teams and to provide meaningful rewards and incentives.

In addition to creating an environment of trust and respect, leaders in the Growth Environment should also focus on creating an atmosphere of learning and growth. This means that leaders must be willing to empower their team members and allow them to make mistakes. When mistakes are made, leaders should work with their team members to learn from the mistake and create an action plan for improvement. They should also recognize and reward successful efforts and progress.

To foster a Growth Environment, leaders must also be willing to take risks and embrace change. Leaders should be open to trying new things and experimenting with different strategies. Once a strategy has been implemented, it is important to review the results and adjust existing plans or create new ones.

Leaders in the Growth Environment must be willing to lead by example. They should be open and honest with their team members and demonstrate the type of behavior they wish to see. They should also be willing to take responsibility for their mistakes and create an environment where mistakes are seen as a learning opportunity rather than a source of shame.

The Growth Environment is an effective model for leadership because it encourages learning from mistakes, rewards creativity, and celebrates the successes of all team members. It emphasizes the importance of open communication, trust, and respect, and nurtures collaboration, innovation, and problem-solving. Leaders who foster a Growth Environment will be able to create an atmosphere of trust, respect, and learning, while also promoting growth and innovation within their organization.

Creating momentum for a business with a growth mentality is an essential part of achieving success in any given industry. By learning from mistakes and using them as an opportunity for growth, businesses can develop a culture of innovation and resilience that leads to success. This type of approach is especially useful for businesses that are looking to break into new markets or develop products and services that are new and disruptive.

One of the most important elements of creating momentum for a business with a growth mentality is learning from mistakes and using them as an opportunity for growth. This means accepting mistakes as part of the process, acknowledging them, and then using them to determine the best way forward. There are many examples of companies that have done this successfully, ranging from small startups to multinational corporations. One of the most notable examples is DreamWorks, who experienced a period of failure before they were able to create successes such as Shrek and Kung Fu Panda. By learning from their mistakes and not giving up, they were eventually able to create one of the most successful animation studios in the world.

Another way to create momentum for a business with a growth mentality is to create a culture of learning and experimentation. This can be done by encouraging employees to take risks, trying out new ideas, and using data to inform decision-making. This allows businesses to quickly identify what works and what does not, allowing them to pivot and make changes as needed. This type of culture also encourages employees to think outside the box and come up with innovative solutions that can be tested and iterated quickly.

A third way to create momentum for a business with a growth mentality is to focus on customer feedback and use it as a tool for improvement. This means actively seeking out customer feedback, listening to it, and using it to inform decisions. Companies like Amazon use customer feedback to inform their product development decisions and to stay ahead of the competition. This allows them to quickly identify customer needs and respond to them in a timely manner, leading to better products and customer satisfaction.

Another way to create momentum for a business with a growth mentality is to set ambitious goals and be willing to take risks to reach those goals. This means taking calculated risks and investing in new technologies, ideas, and products that may not always work out. Companies like Apple and Tesla are examples of this, as they have taken risks and invested in new technologies that have ultimately paid off. This type of approach requires a certain level of risk-taking, but it can pay off tremendously in the long run.

Creating momentum for a business with a growth mentality requires a combination of all the above strategies. It is essential for businesses to learn from their mistakes, foster a culture of learning, use customer feedback to inform decisions and be willing to take risks to achieve their goals. By doing so, businesses can achieve remarkable success and create a culture of innovation, resilience, and growth that will benefit all stakeholders in the long run.

5 SETTING THE STAGE FOR GROWTH

Humans have been using feedback loops to communicate and grow since the dawn of time. From cave drawings to family conversations, feedback loops have been a key component in the development of communication and emotional intelligence. A feedback loop is a continuous cycle of communication between two or more parties, where the sender of the message receives a response from the receiver, which in turn influences and shapes the next message. Through this process, the parties involved can gain better insights into the thoughts and feelings of one another and can work together to achieve a common goal.

Feedback loops are essential to the development of healthy relationships between people, as they help individuals learn to process, reflect on, and act on insights and information. They also facilitate trust and understanding between people and enable the sharing of ideas and resources. In the workplace, feedback loops are often used to monitor and improve performance. They enable employees to gain an understanding of how their work is viewed and how they can improve their performance.

The success of a feedback loop depends on the clarity and accuracy of the information being communicated. A lack of clarity or inaccuracy can lead to misunderstandings and misinformation. It is important that the sender of the message communicates their message in a way that the receiver can easily understand and make sense of. The communication should also be honest and respectful.

When providing feedback, it is important to ensure that the receiver can fully express their thoughts and feelings. This is key to building trust and understanding between the sender and the receiver. Additionally, it is important to ensure that the feedback given is effective and useful. Feedback should have a positive tone and focus on the recipient's strengths, rather than weaknesses. This will help to promote open dialogue and encourage the recipient to take ownership of their actions.

The ability to effectively receive and deliver feedback is an important component of emotional intelligence. It is important for individuals to be able to understand the feedback that they are receiving, as well as be able to accurately deliver feedback to others. In order to effectively receive feedback, it is important to remain open-minded and remain non-judgmental. It is also important to be able to interpret the messages that are being communicated and to question any statements that are unclear or inaccurate.

The ability to deliver feedback effectively is also an important aspect of emotional intelligence. It is important to be able to communicate clearly and accurately and to ensure that the recipient is able to understand the message that is being communicated. Additionally, it is important to ensure that the feedback is delivered respectfully and positively. This will help to create an atmosphere of trust and understanding between the sender and the receiver.

Perception is also an important factor in the success of a feedback loop. The receiver must be able to accurately interpret the message that is being sent in order to effectively use the feedback. The sender needs to be aware of the receiver's perception, as this will influence the message that is being sent. Additionally, the sender needs to be aware of the receiver's current emotional state in order to ensure that the message is delivered in an appropriate manner.

Overall, feedback loops are essential components of effective communication and emotional intelligence. They provide a platform for individuals to learn from one another and build meaningful relationships. It is important for individuals to be able to effectively receive and deliver feedback in order to create an environment of trust and understanding. Additionally, it is important to ensure that the messages being communicated are clear and accurate and that the receiver is able to accurately interpret the message. It is important to be aware of the receiver's current emotional state in order to ensure that the message is delivered in an appropriate manner.

When discussing coaching it is critical to recognize the need for training on human dynamics and factors so that businesses can better enable leaders to coach their employees. Employee coaching requires an understanding of the individual's psychological makeup. Every employee is different and therefore requires a different approach when it comes to coaching. Employers need to be aware of the individual needs and motivations of their employees to ensure that the coaching program is tailored to them.

When it comes to coaching employees, it is important to understand the psychological factors that influence their behavior. For example, the level of motivation will determine how willing the employee is to learn and take on new tasks. If an employee is not motivated, they are less likely to be receptive to coaching and are more likely to become disengaged. Motivation can be internal or external, so it is important to understand what drives each employee and how to use this to motivate them.

Another important factor to consider when coaching employees is their personality. Each employee will have a unique personality that will affect their behavior and how they respond to different coaching strategies. It is important for employers to be aware of any behavioral patterns that may be present in order for them to effectively coach their employees.

In addition to personality and motivation, it is also important to consider how well an employee is able to handle stress. Some employees may be more prone to stress than others, which can have a negative impact on their performance. It is important to understand how to identify and manage stress to create a positive working environment and ensure that employees are able to perform to the best of their abilities.

For example, some employees may respond well to positive reinforcement, while others may require more intensive coaching and guidance in order to reach their desired performance level. It is also important to remember that each individual has a different set of skills, motivation levels, and interests, and these should be taken into account when coaching to ensure the best possible outcome.

In addition, employers need to be able to recognize the different types of personalities that their employees may possess. For example, some employees may be more introverted while others may be more outgoing. This is an important factor to consider as it will determine how an employer should approach implementing a coaching plan. An employer may have to adapt their coaching style in order to accommodate different types of personalities.

It is also important for employers to recognize the individual strengths and weaknesses of each of their employees. Knowing these strengths and weaknesses can help employers to determine which areas of coaching the employee may need the most assistance with. For example, if an employee is strong in math but weak in communication, it would be beneficial for the employer to focus their coaching efforts on the communication skills of the employee.

One of the most common detractors to successful coaching is the failure to establish a trusting relationship between the employer and the employee. Without a trusting relationship, the employee will most likely be hesitant to open up and discuss their needs and goals with the employer.

Another common detractor to coaching is the lack of communication between the employer and the employee. If the employer does not take the time to discuss the employee's individual needs and goals, the employee is likely to become frustrated and disengaged from the process.

In addition, an employer may also fail to provide clear and consistent feedback to the employee. This lack of feedback can be discouraging to the employee, who may feel like they are not making any progress or are not being adequately supported.

An employer may also fail to recognize the individual strengths and weaknesses of their employees, which can lead to ineffective coaching. If an employer is not aware of the individual needs of their employees, they may not be able to effectively coach them and help them reach their desired performance level.

Employers must become acutely aware of the psychological intricacies of their employees, as well as the subtleties that can impede successful coaching. Extensive training on human dynamics and factors is essential for employers to better equip themselves to help their employees reach their desired performance levels. Employers who fail to go beyond surface-level understanding may find themselves at a loss when attempting to help their staff reach peak results.

Feedback is an essential component of personal and professional growth. It helps individuals understand their strengths and weaknesses, identify areas for improvement, and make necessary changes to achieve their goals. However, giving and receiving feedback can be challenging, especially when people don't feel safe and supported in their environment. Psychological safety and human-centric leadership are two critical concepts that can help create a positive feedback culture and make feedback sessions more effective.

What is Psychological Safety?

Psychological safety refers to the belief that one can speak up without fear of negative consequences. In a psychologically safe environment, people feel comfortable sharing their ideas, opinions, and concerns, knowing that they will be heard and respected. This sense of safety promotes open communication, collaboration, and innovation, which ultimately leads to better outcomes.

Research has shown that psychological safety is crucial for effective feedback sessions. When people feel safe and supported, they are more likely to be receptive to feedback, take it seriously, and act on it. On the other hand, when people feel threatened or judged, they may become defensive, dismissive, or resistant to feedback, which can hinder their growth and development.

Creating a psychologically safe environment requires intentional effort from leaders and team members.

Some ways to promote psychological safety in feedback sessions include:

Creating Psychological Safety in an organization is critical to empowering employees to improve their performance. Psychological safety has four levels. Inclusive safety, Learning Safety, Contribution Safety, and Challenge Safety. Clearly stating expectations and constantly coaching leaders to lead better and employees to perform better can help with creating safety in the organization. Most people believe that psychological safety implies a lack of accountability, but it is the opposite if it is done correctly.

Offering feedback to employees honors the psychological safety that can only be achieved when there is a clear mutual understanding of situations and feelings. Providing feedback also increases their autonomy by giving them more information about your expectations.

A great example of this is illustrated below and is a real-life example with the names changed.

As the CEO of a major corporation, Sarah knew that creating a safe and inclusive workplace was essential to her employees' productivity and well-being. She had worked hard to implement the coaching strategy of the 5 T's and had seen great results in her team's performance.

One morning, Sarah received a complaint from one of her employees, Maria, about a colleague's inappropriate behavior towards her. Sarah immediately called a meeting with both employees to discuss the issue and find a solution.

During the meeting, Sarah noticed that Maria seemed uncomfortable and hesitant to speak up. She realized that

Maria may not feel safe enough to express herself fully in the workplace. Sarah knew that she needed to take action to address this and create a culture of psychological safety.

After the meeting, Sarah called Maria into her office for a one-on-one conversation. She started by apologizing for any discomfort Maria had experienced and asked her to share her thoughts and feelings about the incident.

Maria opened up and shared her concerns about how her colleague's behavior had made her feel and how it had affected her work. Sarah listened intently and assured Maria that her feelings were valid and that she would take action to ensure that this kind of behavior was not tolerated in the workplace.

Sarah provided Maria with feedback and guidance, emphasizing the importance of open communication and mutual understanding. She made it clear to Maria that she had her full support and that she would be there to help her navigate any future issues.

Thanks to Sarah's proactive approach, Maria felt heard, valued, and safe in her workplace. Sarah's commitment to creating a culture of psychological safety not only benefited Maria but also improved the overall performance and morale of her team.

Psychological safety has a compounding effect that is only recently being studied. As you take your teams through the coaching process and constantly provide feedback to them, leaders should always keep psychological safety at the forefront of their minds. If they can create a high accountability and high psychological safety environment, that is the nominal environment for success and growth.

Acknowledge the importance of psychological safety: Leaders should make it clear that psychological safety is a priority and create a culture that values open communication, constructive feedback, and continuous learning.

Listen actively: Leaders should listen actively to feedback and encourage others to do the same. Active listening involves paying attention to what is being said, asking questions, and paraphrasing to ensure understanding. This shows that feedback is valued and respected.

Encourage respectful communication: Leaders should promote respectful communication by modeling it themselves and setting clear expectations for team members. This includes avoiding personal attacks, focusing on behaviors rather than individuals, and using a tone that is respectful and supportive.

Embrace vulnerability: Leaders should be willing to show vulnerability by admitting mistakes, asking for help, and being open to feedback. This helps create a safe space for others to do the same.

Provide regular feedback: Regular feedback helps normalize the feedback process and reduces the fear and anxiety that can come with infrequent feedback. It also provides opportunities for growth and development.

What is Human-Centric Leadership?

Human-centric leadership is an approach that prioritizes the needs and well-being of individuals over the goals of the organization. This type of leadership recognizes that people are the heart of the organization and that their success and happiness are critical to the success of the business.

Human-centric leaders create environments

where people feel valued, supported, and empowered to do their best work. They focus on building strong relationships with team members, understanding their strengths and weaknesses, and providing opportunities for growth and development.

In the context of feedback sessions, human-centric leaders can make a significant difference by:

Building trust: Human-centric leaders prioritize building trust with team members. They do this by being transparent, keeping promises, and being reliable. When trust is established, team members feel more comfortable sharing their thoughts and ideas.

Empowering team members: Human-centric leaders give team members the autonomy and resources they need to succeed. This includes providing feedback and coaching, but also giving them the freedom to make their own decisions and take ownership of their work.

Fostering a growth mindset: Human-centric leaders promote a growth mindset by encouraging team members to view feedback as an opportunity for learning and growth. They help team members identify their strengths and weaknesses and provide guidance on how to improve.

Celebrating successes: Human-centric leaders celebrate successes with team members, recognizing their contributions and accomplishments. This creates a sense of pride and motivation that can help drive continued growth and development.

Coaching is a powerful tool for providing employees with feedback and helping them grow and develop. It involves a one-on-one conversation between a coach and an employee, where the coach provides guidance, support, and feedback on the employee's performance.

To implement coaching in an environment to provide employees with feedback, here are some steps to follow:

Step 1: Establish a coaching culture

To create a coaching culture, leaders need to communicate the importance of coaching and create a supportive environment where coaching is encouraged and valued. This can be done by setting expectations for coaching, providing training and resources for coaches, and recognizing and rewarding coaching efforts.

Step 2: Identify coaches

Identify coaches who have the skills and experience to provide effective coaching. This can be done by looking for individuals who have a track record of success, are good communicators, and are respected by their peers.

Step 3: Set goals and expectations

Set clear goals and expectations for coaching sessions, including the purpose of the coaching, the topics to be covered, and the desired outcomes. This will help ensure that coaching sessions are focused and productive.

Step 4: Prepare for coaching sessions

Before coaching sessions, coaches should prepare by reviewing the employee's performance, identifying areas for improvement, and planning how to provide feedback and guidance. This preparation will help coaches provide targeted and actionable feedback.

Step 5: Conduct coaching sessions

During coaching sessions, coaches should listen actively, provide feedback, and help employees develop action plans for improvement. It's essential to create a safe and supportive environment where employees feel comfortable sharing their thoughts and concerns.

Step 6: Follow up and track progress

Follow-up with employees after coaching sessions to ensure that they are making progress towards their goals. Provide ongoing support and feedback to help them continue to grow and develop.

Benefits of coaching for feedback:

Personalized feedback: Coaching provides employees with personalized feedback tailored to their individual needs and goals. This can help them improve more quickly and effectively.

Increased motivation: Coaching can help employees feel more engaged and motivated by providing them with support and guidance.

Better communication: Coaching sessions can help improve communication between employees and their coaches, as well as between team members.

Increased productivity: Coaching can help employees develop new skills and improve their performance, leading to increased productivity and better outcomes.

Improved job satisfaction: Coaching can help employees feel more fulfilled in their roles by providing them with opportunities for growth and development.

Implementing coaching into an environment to provide employees with feedback can be a powerful way to promote growth and development. By establishing a coaching culture, identifying coaches, setting clear goals and expectations, preparing for coaching sessions, conducting coaching sessions, and following up and tracking progress, organizations can create a supportive environment where employees feel valued and supported. The benefits of coaching for feedback include personalized feedback, increased motivation, better communication, increased productivity, and improved job satisfaction.

6 COACHING FOR INVESTMENT OF HUMAN CAPITAL

The quote "The Culture of any organization is shaped by the worst behavior the leader demonstrates or is willing to allow" signifies the importance of coaching the leaders of a business. If leaders display behavior contrary to the intended culture shift, then the culture change is doomed.

Leadership is the foundation of any successful organization. The culture of any organization is largely shaped by the behavior of its leaders, and for this reason, it is essential for leaders to be coached. Good leadership involves investing in the personal growth and development of employees, setting an example of excellence, motivating and inspiring employees to reach their full potential, and effectively managing and inspiring the team toward success. Coaching leaders can help them to become more effective and successful in their roles, create a more positive, productive working environment, and set a strong foundation for the organization's success.

Coaching is a process of helping people to identify and reach their potential. It is based on the idea that everyone has the potential to learn, grow, and develop to reach their full potential. Coaching has been shown to be an effective tool for improving the performance of employees, especially leaders. Through coaching, leaders can learn new skills, identify and overcome weaknesses, and develop new strategies for leading their teams. Coaching also provides an opportunity for leaders to receive feedback, build relationships with employees, and gain insight into their work culture and environment.

There are various ways in which leaders can be coached. One of the most common methods is through one-on-one coaching sessions. These sessions provide a space for the leader and coach to work together, identify goals, analyze performance, and develop strategies for improvement. Coaches can also use role-playing and other interactive activities to allow the leader to practice new skills and behaviors in a safe environment. Another popular option for leaders is to participate in team coaching sessions, which allow the team to work together to identify areas of improvement, develop strategies, and build relationships.

Another way that leaders can be coached is through professional development training. Professional development training can provide leaders with the skills and knowledge they need to manage their teams more effectively and motivate their employees. Training can cover topics such as communication, conflict resolution, time management, decision-making, and problem-solving. Professional development training also allows leaders to gain insight into the unique dynamics of their teams, understand the needs and motivations of their employees, and develop strategies for managing and leading more effectively.

Coaching is also a valuable tool for helping leaders to build strong relationships with their employees. Leaders who take the time to coach their employees can help to create an environment of trust, respect, and collaboration. Coaches can provide leaders with the skills and strategies they need to help their employees build relationships, foster a sense of belonging, and collaborate to reach goals. This type of coaching also helps to create a culture of open communication, which can be beneficial for the entire organization.

Effective coaching is an essential tool for helping leaders to create an effective working environment. Coaches can provide leaders with strategies for dealing with difficult employees, managing stress, and creating an environment of trust, respect, and collaboration. Coaching can also provide leaders with the tools they need to build strong, productive teams. Through coaching, leaders can learn how to cultivate an environment of accountability, provide effective feedback, and create an atmosphere of collaboration and support.

Effective leaders are not born, they are forged through a crucible of fire and honed into sharp blades that cut through the toughest challenges. Coaching is the hammer that shapes these blades, tempering them into resilient structures that can weather any storm. It is the only way to transform mediocre leaders into inspiring visionaries who can rally their troops toward victory.

Leaders who refuse coaching are doomed to

fail, their egos blinding them to their own weaknesses. But those who embrace it will discover a wellspring of knowledge and insight that opens new horizons. Coaching helps leaders improve their performance and build strong relationships with employees, creating an effective working environment where dreams become reality.

With coaching, leaders become examples of excellence that inspire their subordinates, guiding them through even the most harrowing of trials. They learn how to manage and lead their teams toward success, transforming their organizations from good to great. Coaching is not just valuable - it is essential for anyone seeking true greatness.

The importance of professional development for leaders to retain employees and gain a more engaged workforce is a critical factor of success in any business. Professional development is the process of acquiring new skills, knowledge, and abilities through learning and practice, with the goal of improving performance and increasing a person's value to their organization. Leaders who focus on investing in their people through professional development can create a positive environment that fosters growth and development in each employee, resulting in a more engaged and empowered workforce.

Effective professional development in the workplace begins with a leader's commitment to providing their employees with the opportunity to grow professionally. Leaders should understand the importance of investing in their staff and recognize the invaluable benefits it offers. Investing in professional development can create an environment of trust and respect, as well as an environment where employees feel they are valued and respected. It also helps to build a strong team, as people who feel supported and trusted will be more likely to work together towards a common goal. Furthermore, investing in professional development can help to increase employee morale, as employees who feel they are continuously learning new skills and knowledge are more likely to be motivated and engaged in their work. Finally, providing professional development opportunities for employees can help to retain them, as employees who feel their skills and knowledge are being developed will be more likely to stay with their organization for the long term.

When it comes to professional development, it is important for leaders to be mindful of the type of opportunities they offer their employees. It is important to understand the unique needs and interests of each employee and to tailor professional development opportunities that are suited to their individual needs. This might include providing opportunities for cross-training, allowing employees to attend conferences or workshops related to their field, or offering mentorship opportunities. Leaders should also be mindful of budgeting for professional development and ensuring that employees have access to resources such as books, online courses, or software.

Leaders should also prioritize professional development by recognizing employees' achievements and providing feedback regularly. This helps to ensure employees are on the right track when it comes to their development and can provide them with the motivation to continue striving for improvement. Additionally, leaders should explore ways to offer flexible professional development opportunities such as online courses, lunchtime learning sessions, or team-based learning. This allows employees to develop their skills in their own time and can help to create a learning environment that encourages collaboration and teamwork.

It is important for leaders to be mindful of the impact that professional development has on their organization. Investing in the professional development of employees can help to increase their value to the organization and can help to create a culture of learning and growth. Additionally, investing in professional development can help to create a workforce that is more engaged and motivated, resulting in improved productivity and higher performance. Professional development can also help to attract and retain talented employees, as employees who feel supported and valued in their organization are more likely to stay with the organization for the long term.

Investing in professional development is essential for leaders to retain their employees and gain a more engaged workforce. Leaders should be mindful of their employees' individual needs and interests and provide tailored professional development opportunities that are suited to those needs. Additionally, leaders should prioritize professional development and be mindful of the impact it has on their organization. Professional development can create an environment of trust and respect and can help to increase employee morale and performance, attract and retain talented employees, and create a culture of learning and growth. Investing in professional development is an essential part of any successful organization and should be a top priority for all leaders.

Human capital is an incredibly valuable asset to businesses, yet it is often overlooked or undervalued. Investing in people can have a direct and positive impact on the bottom line, but it is an investment that is often neglected in favor of more tangible assets such as equipment and property. It is a mistake to think of people as a cost to a business, as the cost of investing in human capital is far outweighed by the gains to be made from creating a dynamic and motivated workforce.

The term 'human capital' refers to the knowledge, skills, and abilities of a person, and how they can be applied to create value for a business. It is important to remember that people are the driving force of any business, and the investments made in their development should reflect this fact. Investing in human capital is not simply about increasing the number of workers or reducing the cost of labor. It is about investing in the potential of the people and developing the skills they need to succeed in their roles.

Employing skilled and well-trained staff is essential for businesses as it improves efficiency, productivity, and customer service. When staff is well-trained and motivated, they can produce high-quality work more quickly and with less waste. This improves customer satisfaction, ultimately leading to increased sales and profit.

Investing in human capital can also lead to greater staff retention. It is far more cost-effective to invest in the development of existing staff to help them reach their full potential than to constantly employ and train new staff to replace those that have left. Providing employees with the means to develop their skills can also help to create a culture of trust and loyalty in the workplace, leading to increased job satisfaction and commitment to the company.

A well-trained, motivated, and loyal workforce also helps to increase the overall public perception of a company. Investing in human capital can help to create a positive image of the company as a responsible employer that values its staff and is committed to their development. This can help to attract more customers and potential employees, increasing the overall profitability of the business.

In terms of financial gain, investing in human capital can be highly beneficial. Training and development of staff can increase the productivity of the workforce, thus increasing the profits of the business. Additionally, as staff becomes more skilled and experienced, they can often take on higher levels of responsibility, leading to increased job satisfaction and career progression. This can result in increased staff retention, reducing the costs associated with the recruitment and training of new staff.

Investing in human capital can also lead to greater innovation and creativity within the workforce, as staff is allowed to develop their skills and knowledge. As staff are given more opportunities to learn new skills and ideas, they can bring a fresh perspective to the company, leading to the development of new products and services. This can, in turn, lead to increased sales and profits for the business.

When investing in human capital, businesses should ensure that the investment is targeted, measurable, and sustainable. Training and development initiatives should be designed to achieve specific goals, such as improving customer service or increasing the efficiency of the workplace. Businesses should also measure the impact of the investment in terms of the number of staff that have been trained and the degree to which it has improved efficiency and profit. Finally, businesses should ensure that their investment in human capital is sustainable and that training and development initiatives are reviewed and updated regularly in order to keep staff up to date with the latest developments in their areas of expertise

7 EFFECTIVE ELEMENTS WITHIN A COACHING SESSION

The effectiveness of a coaching interaction with an employee is determined by the success of the outcome. If a coach can develop meaningful relationships with the employees and help them to reach their goals, then the relationship is considered successful. Coaching is a form of development and growth through honest dialogue, feedback, guidance, and encouragement from the coach. The key elements of successful coaching are developing trust, creating a safe and open environment, providing feedback, setting goals and expectations, and helping the employee to stay motivated and engaged.

Creating Trust

The first and foremost element of a

successful coaching interaction is trust. Trust between a coach and their employee is essential for a constructive coaching relationship as it allows employees to feel comfortable with their coach and to share their thoughts openly. Although trust is important in all relationships, for one's boss to be able to trust that an employee can do their job well enough without supervision and follow through on the tasks assigned is crucial for measuring performance. In order for employees to trust the coach, they must feel respected and accepted by them. To build trust with an employee, there are three possible routes a coach can take: sharing information, providing support, and helping improve skills. The first step towards building a relationship with an employee is creating open channels of communication by asking questions and listening attentively. An effective question stays focused on one topic, such as work or family, instead of being broad or tangential (which may make an employee feel like they are being interrogated). Once the employee feels comfortable speaking about themselves and working with their coach, then the possibilities for enhancing trust increase. For example, if an employee has been having difficulty understanding how to manage multiple projects effectively, allow them to explain what they have found difficult or challenging. By offering up some general advice and insights based on their own experience, the coach can help alleviate some of the stress associated with the task and demonstrate expertise in the role of manager.

Creating a Safe and Open Environment

Creating a safe and open environment for employees to discuss their issues and ideas is another key element of a successful coaching interaction. In order to make employees feel comfortable, the coach needs to provide a physical and psychological environment that is supportive and non-judgmental. Employees should be able to express themselves without fear of being judged or reprimanded. The coach should also ensure that the environment is free from distractions and that the focus is on addressing the issues at hand.

Providing Feedback

Providing feedback is a crucial part of a successful coaching interaction. The coach needs to provide feedback that is clear and honest, but also sensitive and constructive. The feedback should be tailored to the individual needs of the employee and should not be overly critical. The goal of the feedback should be to give the employee a better understanding of their strengths and weaknesses and to provide them with the information they need to improve their performance.

Setting Goals and Expectations

Setting goals and expectations is an important part of coaching. The coach should work with the employee to set achievable goals that are aligned with the objectives of the organization. The coach should also ensure that the employee is aware of the expectations that come with achieving these goals. This will help to provide the employee with a sense of direction and purpose, allowing them to stay focused and motivated.

Helping the Employee to Stay Motivated and Engaged

The final element of a successful coaching interaction is helping the employee to stay motivated and engaged. The coach should be able to recognize and appreciate the employee's efforts and provide them with encouragement and support. This can be done by providing the employee with positive feedback, recognizing their achievements, and offering them opportunities for growth and development. The coach should also be able to provide resources and tools that can help the employee reach their goals.

These five elements – trust, creating a safe and open environment, providing feedback, setting goals and expectations, and helping the employee to stay motivated and engaged – are essential for a successful coaching interaction. By focusing on these elements, a coach can help employees to reach their goals and become more successful in their careers.

Basic Coaching interactions (Not talking

Performance improvement plans) should include observed behavior, environment expectations, action plans, follow-up scheduling, feedback opportunity for the person being coached, and asking for any support that is needed. These steps help to ensure that both the coach and the person being coached are able to work together to create an environment of support, growth, and success.

Observed Behavior

The first step in the coaching process is to observe the behavior of the person being coached. This includes noting their body language, facial expressions, and any other non-verbal communication. It is also beneficial to observe how the person interacts with others and their environment as this can provide insight into their thoughts, feelings, and needs. Additionally, the coach should note any areas that the person is succeeding in and any areas they are struggling with, as this will help to create a plan of action.

Environment Expectations

When beginning the coaching process, it is important to establish expectations for both parties in terms of the environment. This includes setting ground rules, such as respecting each other's opinions and agreeing to confidentiality. It is also important to establish a safe space where the person being coached can express their feelings without feeling judged or criticized. This can include providing a space for conversations that is free from distractions, as well as a time limit to ensure that conversations stay productive and on track.

Action Plans

Once the behavior has been observed and the expectations for the environment have been set, the coach and the person being coached can work together to create action plans for achieving their goals. This should include setting measurable and achievable goals, as well as identifying the steps that need to be taken to achieve them. This could include creating a timeline with deadlines for each step, as well as assigning specific tasks or activities to the person being coached. Additionally, it is important to discuss any potential obstacles that may arise and how to best overcome them.

Follow Up Scheduling

In order to ensure progress is being made, it is important to schedule regular follow-up meetings. This allows both the coach and the person being coached to review progress, discuss any changes that may have been made, and make any necessary adjustments to the action plan. Additionally, follow-up meetings allow the coach to provide feedback and guidance, as well as to ensure the person being coached is feeling supported throughout the process.

Feedback Opportunity

Throughout the coaching process, it is important to provide the person being coached with opportunities to receive feedback. This could include having weekly check-in meetings to review progress and give feedback or providing regular written or verbal feedback about their progress. Additionally, feedback can be provided throughout the process, with the coach providing both positive feedback for successes and constructive criticism for areas that need improvement. This helps to ensure that the person being coached can make adjustments and stay on track toward their goals.

Ask for Support

Finally, it is important to ask the person being coached if they need any additional support during the coaching process. This could include providing additional resources or referrals, scheduling additional meetings to review progress, or creating a plan to address any areas that may need additional work. Additionally, the coach should be open to any suggestions the person being coached may have in terms of additional resources or support that could help them reach their goals.

Coaching is a unique form of teaching and mentorship that is designed to help individuals and teams reach their peak performance. It is a process that requires consistency, effort, and dedication to be successful. Just as going to the gym to stay in shape requires consistent effort, effective coaching requires sustained effort as well.

The difference between coaching and going to the gym is that the latter is usually focused on improving a person's physical health and physical appearance, whereas the former is usually focused on improving a person's mental and emotional health, as well as their skills and abilities. Both processes require the individual to be committed and focused to see improvement and progress, but it is important to remember that the coaching process is about more than just improving performance. It is about helping individuals grow and to become a better version of themselves.

Just like going to the gym, the coaching process is about developing a routine that works for you. Each individual or team is unique, and so the coach must be able to adapt their approach to fit each individual and team's unique needs and challenges. This could include setting realistic goals, providing feedback and guidance, and designing an environment that encourages learning and growth.

A successful coach is someone who truly understands their client's needs, their strengths and weaknesses, and their overall objectives. They must be able to create a plan that will help their client reach their peak performance, and they must be able to adjust their approach and strategies as the client's goals and situation change. A successful coach is also someone who is able to motivate their client and help them stay focused and motivated over the long term, and this requires creating an environment that is supportive and encouraging.

Just like going to the gym, the coaching process requires consistency and sustained effort in order to see results. It is important to remember that it will take time to reach the desired goals and that the process will require ongoing effort and dedication in order to see real results. A coach must be able to push their client beyond their comfort zone, and they must be able to provide support and guidance at all times. It is also important to remember that coaching is not a "quick fix" and that it takes time and dedication in order to see a difference in the individual or team being coached.

The comparison between coaching and going to the gym can be seen in the way that both require a commitment to a process over time. Just as going to the gym requires consistent effort and dedication, so does the coaching process. Both require the individual or team to make a commitment to their success, and both require the individual or team to push themselves beyond their comfort zone in order to reach their peak performance.

8 DEFINING AND COMMUNICATING A STANDARD PLAN

The need for a structured system of coaching and mentoring is becoming increasingly pertinent in the professional world. Coaching and mentoring have been used for centuries and have been found to be invaluable resources in helping individuals to develop their skills and reach their goals. Coaching and mentoring can be used to help people to increase their productivity, become better leaders, and to develop the necessary skills to secure their future success. The benefits of having a structured system in place are clear, however, to make this system effective, it must be followed consistently and tracked accordingly.

As James Clear, author of Atomic Habits has stated, "You do not rise to the level of your goals. You fall to the level of your systems." This quote emphasizes the importance of having a system in place and following it consistently rather than simply having a goal. It is the system that will be the key element in reaching the goal.

The system that will be covered in the module today is what we will affectionately call the 5 T approach. Using the 5 T's (Teaching, Train, Trust/Thrive, Transfer, Terminate) provides structure and a way to track progress. Teaching, Train, and Trust/Thrive all involve different aspects of the coaching and mentoring system. There are two direct pathways that team members can be coached using this 5 T approach. There is a possibility for a third. Due to this potential for redemption, I believe this is the most empathetic approach to coaching and allows the team member to provide feedback at multiple steps and when they veer off course, it allows the manager multiple paths to correct them.

The pathways I see are as follows;

Teach - Train - Trust/Thrive

Teach - Train - Trust/Thrive - Transfer – Trust/Thrive

Team – Train – Trust/Thrive - Transfer – Terminate

The system of using a 5T methodology has been very successful and increased retention when used properly. This system is a conglomerate mix of different psychological approaches to coaching. Utilizing the adult learning cycle this method allows the person to train under other than nominal conditions and gives the person multiple chances to provide feedback or alert their leader of issues.

Using a system such as the 5 T's will help to

ensure that the coaching and mentoring process follows a structured path and can be tracked. It will also help to ensure that all of the necessary steps are taken and that the individual is prepared to end the relationship when the time comes. Additionally, having a system in place will help to ensure that the relationship is a successful one and that the individual is being properly trained and developed.

The key strategy that will be reviewed in this book for coaching is the 5 T method. This method is useful and highly effective in real-life business environments. This method is successful whether in an office, manufacturing, or transactional environment, and can be used at all levels of the organization.

The 5 T's are Teach, Train, Trust, Thrive, Transfer, and Terminate. The definitions of each are as follows:

Teaching: This involves imparting knowledge and skills to the individual being coached. The coach must have a thorough understanding of the subject matter and be able to effectively communicate the information to the person being coached.

Train: This involves practicing and reinforcing the skills that have been taught. The coach should provide opportunities for the person being coached to put the knowledge into practice and offer feedback to help them improve.

Trust/Thrive: This involves building a relationship of mutual trust and respect between the coach and the person being coached. The coach should act as a mentor and provide support and encouragement to help the individual reach their potential.

This also involves creating an environment that fosters growth and development. The coach should help the person being coached to set goals and develop a plan for achieving them, as well as provide motivation and accountability to help them stay on track.

Transfer: This involves transferring the person to another department or section in the organization. This should be done when there is not sufficient progress made through the first three T's. This should also only be done if the person shows relevant skills or intangible qualities that could benefit the company.

Termination: Termination from a job refers to the end of an individual's employment with a particular business or company. This process may be voluntary or involuntary. In a voluntary termination, the employee decides to leave the job. In an involuntary termination, the employer decides to end the individual's employment.

The benefit of having a rigid structured system like the 5T's (Teaching, Train, Trust, Thrive, Transfer, and Terminate) is that everyone in the organization will be required to go through some of them. If we, as leaders, do this right, our teams will be taught, and trained, we will trust in them, and they will thrive. Hopefully, very rarely will we have to use the final two T's of Transfer and Terminate.

By creating an environment where there is consistency and a system, we can make sure that our team members are aware of what is expected of them and how they can succeed in their roles. It is essential to communicate these expectations clearly to avoid confusion or misunderstandings.

However, when it comes to the transfer and termination of team members, it is crucial to handle these situations delicately and with great care. Transferring a team member may be necessary if their skills or expertise would be better utilized in a different department or project. In such cases, it is important to communicate the reasons for the transfer and help the team members make a smooth transition to their new roles.

Termination, on the other hand, is something that should only be used as a last resort. If a team member is not meeting the performance expectations despite proper teaching, training, trust, and support, termination may be necessary. However, it is essential to ensure that the reasons for termination are communicated clearly and empathetically to the team members and to do everything possible to help them find closure within the communication process.

Communicating the structured process of the

5T's (Teaching, Train, Trust, Thrive, Transfer, Terminate) is a key step to beginning a consistent process that will last as the person progresses through the steps. This communication should be standardized and documented at the beginning of employment.

The importance of stating expectations and goals cannot be overstated. It sets the foundation for a successful work relationship between employer and employee. It also helps to ensure that everyone is on the same page and has a clear understanding of what is expected of them.

Communicating expectations should be done clearly and concisely. It's important to use precise language and avoid ambiguity. This will help to prevent misunderstandings and ensure that everyone is aware of what's expected of them.

In addition to clearly stating expectations and goals, it's also important to provide proper periodic feedback, communication, and support. This will help employees to develop the necessary skills and knowledge to perform their jobs effectively.

Trust is another important component of the 5T's process. Employers must be able to trust their employees to fulfill their responsibilities and meet expectations. This trust can be started to be built through open communication, transparency, and a willingness to listen and provide feedback. The initial conversation about expectations is a great place to start building trust and psychological safety with your team.

When employees feel supported, cared for, psychologically safe, and valued, they are more likely to thrive in their roles. This can lead to increased productivity, job satisfaction, and a positive work environment.

Ultimately, the goal of the 5T's process is to clearly define expectations, provide a system of coaching so that it is standardized, and empower teams to take ownership of their roles and drive success for the organization

9 TEACHING

Teaching is the first in the process of the 5 T's. Teaching is at the base of where we start with each one of our team members. Team members can bring task-related skills to our organization, but we must teach everyone job-specific skills. It is important to remember where everyone starts. The learning environment can be very stressful, and this is critical for leaders to define the teaching environment.

Teaching involves empathy. The teacher is not only teaching them job-specific tasks but also about culture and the work environment.

As a new leader in my early roles, I can say that I did not always do the best job of this. At first, I created an environment where new team members were met with a mentality of performing or would be terminated. I could not see at the time, but this was creating added stress that was detracting from their ability to learn. This made it harder for the new employees to learn and prolonged the training period as well as driving a low retention rate.

When I started researching the benefits of psychological safety in an environment and the power an environment had over the behaviors of people in it, I was inspired to change. I changed the entire system of onboarding to become more empathetic and clearly defined that I understood the new employees were going to make mistakes and it was ok to make the mistakes if we learned from them. I saw that it was critically important for me to create a safe and welcoming environment for my new team members. I wanted to make sure that they felt comfortable asking questions and making mistakes. My leadership team drove psychological safety into the environment, normalized mistakes, and provided regular and concise feedback. We changed our mentality so that we could make sure to approach teaching with empathy and understanding.

As a leader, I started by taking the time to get to know each team member individually. I wanted to understand their background, strengths, and weaknesses. This allowed me to tailor my teaching approach to each individual, making sure that they were receiving the necessary support and guidance to succeed.

During our initial training sessions, I made sure to emphasize the importance of our company culture and values. I wanted my team members to understand that they were not just learning a job, but they were also becoming a part of a community. I encouraged open communication, respect, and collaboration.

Teaching skills were just as important as task-related skills. I made sure that my team members understood the "why" behind each task, and how their role fit within the jigsaw puzzle that was our company.

Teaching is an integral part of any successful organization. Not only is it essential to impart knowledge to new employees, but teaching can also help to cultivate and reinforce an organization's culture, vision, and values. The first step in teaching new employees is to help them understand the culture of the organization.

Organizational culture can come in many forms. It can be based on values or goals and can range from very relaxed to highly structured. It is important to understand the culture and message of the organization before a new employee can be properly trained. In order to do this, a supervisor or manager should talk to the new employee about the mission, vision, and values of the organization. This can be done in a formal presentation or group discussion and should be tailored to the size, industry, and type of organization.

The next step in teaching new employees is to provide them with a comprehensive overview of the organization's operations. This should include an introduction to the organizational structure and the roles and responsibilities of those involved. This can be done through group discussions, individual presentations, and/or an introductory training manual. It is important to include both written and visual aids to better communicate the information to the new employee.

Once the new employee is familiar with the structure of the organization, it is important to provide them with a detailed job description. This should include the expected responsibilities of the role, as well as any additional duties that may be added as the organization grows. It is important to provide the employee with a clear understanding of what is expected of them to ensure their success.

Next, it is important to provide the new employee with a thorough explanation of the organization's policies and procedures. This should include an overview of any rules, regulations, or codes of conduct that the employee is expected to adhere to. It is important to ensure that the employee understands these policies and is aware of any potential consequences for non-compliance.

Another key aspect of teaching new employees is to provide them with an understanding of the organization's technology and systems. This should include instruction on how to access and use the organization's computer systems, software applications, and other technology tools. It is also important to provide the new employee with an understanding of any security protocols or procedures necessary to protect the organization's data and systems.

It is important to provide the new employee with an understanding of the organization's customer service and customer relations. This should include an introduction to the organization's customer service philosophy, standards, and procedures. It is important to stress the importance of providing excellent customer service and building positive customer relationships.

Teaching a new employee is an important first step in a new organization. By providing the new employee with a comprehensive understanding of the organization's culture, operations, policies, technology, and customer service, the new employee can become a successful and productive member of the team.

The adult learning cycle is an important tool for any company that wants to ensure that its employees are learning effectively and efficiently. It is an effective way to structure the teaching process so that all of the information that is provided to employees is absorbed, understood, and remembered. The adult learning cycle consists of four stages: preparation, presentation, practice, and assessment. Each stage of the cycle serves a specific purpose and when used correctly, can be an invaluable teaching tool for any organization.

The first stage of the adult learning cycle is preparation. During the preparation stage, the instructor should ensure that the employees have all of the materials necessary to understand and complete the training. This includes books, handouts, and other materials that the employees will need. Additionally, the instructor should also prepare any visual aids, such as slides, diagrams, or videos, that they plan to use during the presentation. This stage is also a good opportunity to get to know the employees and build rapport with them, as this can help to create an atmosphere of trust and open communication.

The next stage of the adult learning cycle is the presentation stage. During this stage, the instructor presents the material to the employees and provides them with an overview of the topic. This is the most important stage of the cycle as it provides the employees with basic knowledge and understanding of the material. The instructor should ensure that the presentation is clear and concise and that the employees are actively engaged in the discussion. This can be done through questions, activities, and other forms of interactive learning.

The third stage of the adult learning cycle is practice. This stage is often overlooked, but it is an essential part of the teaching process. During this stage, the instructor should provide the employees with hands-on opportunities to practice what they have learned. This could include role-playing scenarios, or it could involve working with a partner or in a small group to apply the knowledge they have acquired. Practice is important as it allows the employees to gain a deeper understanding of the material and to develop the skills necessary to apply it in the workplace.

The final stage of the adult learning cycle is assessment. During this stage, the instructor should assess the employees' understanding of the material. This can be done through a variety of methods, such as written tests, oral presentations, or case studies. The assessment should provide the instructor with an understanding of how well the employees have understood and applied the material. It is also an opportunity for the instructor to provide feedback and further guidance to the employees so that they can continue to develop their knowledge and skills.

The adult learning cycle is an effective tool for any company that wants to ensure that its employees are learning effectively and efficiently. By taking the time to provide employees with an effective teaching process, companies can ensure that their employees are well-prepared to meet the demands of the job. Additionally, the use of the adult learning cycle can help to reduce defects and promote increased efficiency in the workplace.

For example, if employees are properly taught how to operate a machine, they are less likely to make errors. This can result in fewer defects and fewer production delays. Additionally, if employees can correctly identify what a defect looks like, they can take the necessary steps to address the issue before it becomes a more significant problem.

Another example is the use of the adult learning cycle to teach employees about safety protocols. When employees are trained and understand the safety rules and regulations of their workplace, they are more likely to abide by them and less likely to be injured on the job. This can result in fewer accidents, fewer workers' compensation claims, and fewer delays in production due to injury or illness.

The use of the adult learning cycle can help to reduce the amount of time employees spend on the job. If employees are properly taught and understand their responsibilities, they are more likely to complete their tasks quickly and efficiently. This can allow companies to complete projects more quickly, resulting in increased productivity and profits.

The adult learning cycle is an essential tool for any company that wants to ensure that its employees are learning effectively and efficiently. By taking the time to properly teach employees, companies can reduce defects, increase safety, and improve productivity in the workplace. Moreover, the use of the adult learning cycle helps to create an environment of trust and open communication between the instructor and the employees, which can further enhance the teaching process.

10 TRAINING

After following the first step of Teaching the new employee (this includes culture, business norms, and job-specific tasks) the next step is to train them. Some people mistake teaching for training. Due to the misconception that surrounds the adult learning cycle, businesses assume that because they "taught" someone a task their job is complete, and if the person does not perform that it is their fault. This is false.

Teaching the task or job is the first step. That is the base level, then you must train them. The teaching step only covers the basics and nominal conditions. The training step covers periodic growth, experience in less than nominal conditions, and the experiences of failure and mistakes. This training step will take some time and should involve regimented training or coaching. There should be periodic check-ins with the employee to get feedback on their performance and how they feel their training is going. These sessions should be frequent enough that the leader could steer the performance before it enters a low-performing state.

As the employee progresses through their training, they should be presented with a task or job to complete. The tasks should start easy and gradually increase in difficulty as the employee becomes more experienced. This will allow them to test their mettle and see how far they have progressed. They should also be given challenges that push them out of their comfort zone to help them grow even further.

The leader must keep up with the progress of the training by providing feedback and guidance when needed. This will help give the employee a sense of accomplishment and will make it easier for them to stay motivated throughout the process. The leader should also provide encouragement and positive reinforcement when an employee succeeds in completing a task or job successfully.

At this point, it is time to evaluate the success of the training program. Evaluations can include surveys, interviews, focus groups, or other methods to get feedback from both employees and leaders on how successful the program has been so far. This data can then be used to make adjustments if necessary, to ensure that everyone involved is getting the maximum benefit from the program.

Without proper training, an individual may never reach their full potential or even come close to achieving their goals. With proper guidance, consistent feedback, and effective evaluation techniques, any individual can become successful at whatever they put their minds to!

Once the employee has a good foundation of knowledge and experience, they can be given more autonomy. This may include delegating tasks, allowing them to work with limited supervision, or even giving them projects to complete independently. At this point in their training, it is important to provide feedback on their independent performance and make sure they understand what is expected of them. This can also be an opportunity for the leader to help their employee identify areas for improvement so that they can continue to develop professionally.

When the employee feels confident in their abilities and receives positive feedback from their leader, it is time to move on to the next level of training. This could involve a mentor/mentee relationship or working on more complex tasks with higher levels of responsibility. It is also important for leaders to remember that not every employee learns at the same rate and some may need more guidance or support than others along the way. Leaders must provide support where needed and create an environment that encourages employees to continue learning while still feeling comfortable in their roles.

Training should be ongoing throughout an employee's career, as there will always be room for growth and development no matter how experienced someone becomes in a role. Leaders should plan check-ins periodically throughout an employee's career so that they remain up to date on changes in technology or processes within the organization as well as general industry trends. This will ensure that employees stay current with new developments and have access to any necessary resources they need to succeed.

11 TRUST/THRIVE

Once you have progressed through the teach and train portions of the process the next part is one of the hardest for a leader to do. We must trust our people.

As a leader, trusting your people can be difficult, especially when you've invested so much time and effort into training them. But it's a necessary step in building a successful team.

I learned this lesson the hard way when I was a young business leader. I was micromanaging my employees to the point where they felt suffocated and couldn't perform at their best. It wasn't until I took a step back and trusted them to do their jobs that I saw real growth and success in the company.

One of my employees was particularly talented

but always seemed to be held back by my constant hovering. One day, I decided to give her a project and let her run with it without any interference from me. I was amazed at the results. Not only did she complete the project within the deadline, but she also exceeded my expectations with the quality of her work.

From that day forward, I made a conscious effort to trust my team and give them the space they needed to excel. It wasn't always easy, but it paid off in the end. Our company grew exponentially, and my team became more motivated and engaged in their work.

Trust is a two-way street, however, and it's important to cultivate a culture of openness and honesty in the workplace. By being transparent with my team about my expectations and goals, and by listening to their feedback and concerns, we were able to build a strong foundation of trust and mutual respect.

In the end, I learned that trusting your people is not only necessary for success, but it's also a sign of good leadership. A leader who trusts and empowers their team is one who inspires them to be more and do more.

I believe that in order to foster an environment of trust and honesty, it is essential to have regular conversations with my team. This could be done through daily check-ins for quick updates on progress or simply setting aside time each week for a longer meeting to discuss any challenges the team may be facing. I found that having these discussions allowed us to address any issues head-on and come up with solutions together.

In addition, I made sure to create a supportive atmosphere where everyone felt comfortable expressing their thoughts and ideas without fear of judgment or criticism. This was achieved by fostering collaboration instead of competition, and by allowing everyone an equal opportunity to contribute their ideas and insights. Creating an environment where all members felt respected and their opinions were valued, enabled us to build a strong sense of trust between each other.

I also made sure to reward excellent performance when it was due. Whether it was through verbal praise or more tangible rewards such as bonuses or promotions, rewarding my team for their hard work showed them how much we value their contributions. This further strengthened our level of trust as they knew that I would recognize and reward them for their efforts which motivated them even more.

Overall, building a culture of openness and trust within my team took time but the effort paid off in the end as we were able to achieve great things together because everyone was working towards the same goal with mutual respect for each other's contributions.

As stated before, Trust is a two-way street and if this trust is not being cared for it will die. If you have an employee who is underperforming, then it is your responsibility to keep the lines of communication open so that the team can recover from their low points.

Studying the Pygmalion effect shows us that our expectations of others can greatly impact their performance. As a leader, it's important to have high expectations of your team but also to communicate those expectations clearly and provide the necessary support to help them meet those expectations.

The Pygmalion effect, or Rosenthal effect, is a psychological phenomenon in which high expectations lead to improved performance in a given area and low expectations lead to worse. The effect is named for the Greek myth of Pygmalion, the sculptor who fell so much in love with the perfectly beautiful statue he created that the statue came to life.

The psychologists Robert Rosenthal and Lenore Jacobson, in their book Pygmalion in the Classroom, borrowed something of the myth by advancing the idea that teachers' expectations of their students affect the student's performance, a view that has been called into question because of later research findings.

Rosenthal and Jacobson held that high expectations lead to better performance and low expectations lead to worse, both effects leading to a self-fulfilling prophecy.

According to the Pygmalion effect, the targets of the expectations internalize their positive labels, and those with positive labels succeed; accordingly, a similar process works in the opposite direction in the case of low expectations. The idea behind the Pygmalion effect is that increasing the leader's expectation of the follower's performance will result in better follower performance.

But what happens when trust is broken? It's inevitable that at some point, someone on the team may make a mistake or let us down. In these situations, it's important to address the issue directly and honestly, without placing blame or shaming the individual. Instead, we should focus on finding a solution and working together to prevent similar mistakes in the future.

One of the most challenging aspects of leadership is balancing trust with accountability. We want to trust our team to do their jobs well, but we also need to hold them accountable for their actions and the impact those actions have on the company. This requires clear communication, setting expectations, and following through on consequences when necessary. For this reason, the person can either excel to the next level of Thrive or divert to receive additional coaching in the transfer/terminate zone.

Thriving within a business organization is vital for success. A business organization needs to create a positive and productive working environment where employees can reach their full potential and be successful. This can be a challenge as each person needs to be motivated, can learn and develop, and be part of a successful team. To do this, certain aspects need to be taken into consideration.

The first step to thriving in a business organization is to develop a growth mindset. This means that instead of looking at mistakes, problems, or setbacks as a failure, they should be seen as an opportunity to learn and develop. By having this mindset, employees are more likely to take risks and experiment with new ideas or strategies, which is essential for any organization to be successful. Additionally, it is important that both successes and mistakes are embraced, and that feedback is given positively and constructively. This allows employees to learn from their mistakes and build on their successes.

Having the right tools and resources is also essential for employees to be successful. By providing employees with the necessary tools and resources, such as technology, software, and training materials, they can more effectively and efficiently do their job. Additionally, it is important to ensure that the tools and resources provided are up-to-date and relevant. This is especially important in areas such as information technology, where quickly-evolving technology must be correctly utilized to ensure success.

Another key factor that contributes to an employee's ability to thrive in a business organization is the culture that is created and maintained. This culture should be one of collaboration, respect, and support. Every employee should feel comfortable sharing their ideas and be part of the decision-making process. Additionally, there should be an atmosphere of trust and acceptance, where mistakes are seen as a learning opportunity, and where employees feel free to take risks and experiment with new strategies.

Communication is also an essential part of any successful business organization. Communication must be clear and effective so that everyone is on the same page and working towards the same goals. Regular meetings should be held so that any questions or issues can be discussed and addressed. Additionally, feedback should be given constructively and positively, so that employees can learn from their mistakes and build on their successes.

Effective coaching and mentoring are essential for employees to be successful within a business organization. This can be done through regular one-on-one meetings or group coaching sessions with experienced and knowledgeable staff members. By providing employees with the opportunity to learn from experienced and knowledgeable individuals, they can gain valuable insight and develop the necessary skills to be successful. Additionally, these sessions can be used to discuss any issues or questions that the employees may have, so that they can be addressed and resolved promptly.

Harnessing success in a business organization is essential for long-term growth and stability. Developing a growth mindset, equipping employees with the necessary tools and resources, creating an environment of collaboration and support, effectively communicating opportunities for advancement, and providing coaching and mentoring are all key components to achieving this success. By taking these steps, employees are empowered to thrive and contribute significantly to the ongoing success of the business organization.

When a business takes the time to engage with its employees and create an atmosphere of connection and growth, it can open the door to a thriving business. Employees become more engaged, productive, and committed to the company, leading to higher retention rates and a more enjoyable work environment.

The first step in creating an engaging and productive work environment is to understand the importance of employee engagement. Employee engagement is defined as the emotional commitment of an employee to their work and their organization and is considered to be the foundation of successful businesses. Employee engagement is a key factor in attracting and retaining high-performing employees, as well as promoting productivity, creativity, and innovation.

Once a business understands the importance of employee engagement, it can take steps to create an environment that encourages it.

The first step is to build trust between staff and the business. Employee trust is closely related to engagement, and when staff feels trusted and respected, they are more likely to be productive, innovative, and committed to the organization. Building trust between staff and management can be achieved through effective communication, transparency, and recognition of employees' contributions.

Second, businesses should focus on creating a

sense of belonging. A sense of belonging is important for employees to feel connected to the organization, which will in turn increase engagement and productivity. This can be done by encouraging collaboration between teams, providing recognition for achievements, and creating a culture of inclusion.

Third, businesses should provide employees with opportunities for growth and development. This can be done through training and development programs, career advancement opportunities, and mentorship. By providing these opportunities, employees will feel valued and have the chance to enhance their skills and contribute to the organization.

Fourth, businesses should provide employees with feedback and support. Regular feedback is important for employees to understand how their performance is being evaluated and what areas they need to improve. Regular support from management and peers is also important to help employees build confidence and stay motivated.

Businesses should foster positive relationships with employees. This can be done through open and honest communication, setting clear expectations, and recognizing employees' successes. Employees who feel valued and appreciated are more likely to stay in the organization and be productive.

Taking the time to create an environment that encourages employee engagement can pay off for businesses in the long run. Employees that are engaged and motivated are more likely to stay with the organization and be productive, leading to higher retention rates and more enjoyable work environments.

There are many ways that businesses can create an environment that encourages employee engagement. By understanding the importance of employee engagement, building trust between staff and the business, creating a sense of belonging, providing employees with opportunities for growth and development, providing feedback and support, and fostering positive relationships with employees, businesses can ensure that their employees are motivated, connected, and productive. Doing so will lead to higher retention rates and a more enjoyable work environment for all.

12 TRANSFER/TERMINATE

Employee transfer is an absolute must for organizations looking to get the most out of their staff. Rather than simply accepting poor performance, organizations should be proactive in helping employees capitalize on their skills, talents, and qualities to make a positive contribution to the organization. Those with poor performance can often benefit from being transferred within the organization to areas where their unique set of skills can be best put to use, providing an invaluable tool for both the employee and the organization.

Employee transfer is a process used by organizations to move employees from one job or department to another. This can be done for a variety of reasons, such as to improve productivity, utilize new skills an employee may possess, or address certain performance issues. Employee transfer is an important tool to help employees with poor performance and help the organization make the most of their talents.

There are many benefits to transferring employees within an organization. It can help an organization be more efficient by utilizing the skills and qualities of employees in different capacities. It can also help improve an employee's performance by giving them the opportunity to work in a different environment and be exposed to different challenges. Additionally, transferring employees can help increase job satisfaction, as those who are unhappy in their current role may find a new role more suited to their interests and abilities.

It is important to approach employee transfer with care and consideration. A successful employee transfer requires careful planning and thought. When considering employee transfer, it is important to identify the reasons for the transfer and the potential benefits to both the employee and the organization. The process should include an assessment of the employee's skills, qualities, and performance, as well as a review of their current role and any potential roles they could transfer to. Additionally, it is important to consider the resources available, such as training and support, that could help the employee and the organization make the most of the transfer.

Employee transfer can be a powerful tool for improving performance and driving results. It has been used with great success in numerous cases, where an employee's weaknesses in one role were capitalized on in another. For example, a customer service representative who was struggling to meet their sales goals could be strategically transferred to a technical support role, leveraging their technical expertise and knowledge. Similarly, an ineffective HR specialist who lacked strong interpersonal skills could be moved to a more interactive customer service position, enabling them to use their natural talents to drive success.

Employee transfer can be a powerful weapon in the hands of the organization to deal with employees who fail to meet expectations and maximize the potential of their abilities. It demands meticulous strategizing and evaluation, including a scrutinized analysis of their talents, capacities, and output. Possessing the capacity to tackle performance issues and apply an employee's knowledge and capabilities in different areas, it is evident that employee transfer can be instrumental in bolstering organizational productivity and strengthening lagging employee performance.

The decision to terminate an employee should never be taken lightly, and employers must ensure that they are taking all reasonable steps to ensure that the process is fair and conducted in the best way possible. Terminating an employee can have an enormous impact on both the organization and the individual, and employers must consider the rights of the employee and the impact of dismissal on their reputation.

When considering dismissing an employee, it is important to consider the underlying reasons for the dismissal. It may be the result of a disciplinary issue, or it may be the result of a redundancy situation. In either case, the process should always be handled with empathy and respect for the individual concerned.

When considering terminating an employee, employers should ensure that they follow a fair and reasonable process that meets the employee's rights. This involves providing adequate notice of the dismissal, an opportunity to discuss the issues and any potential options to avoid the dismissal and the documentation of each stage of the process.

It is important that employers recognize the need for fairness and respect when considering terminating an employee. Many countries have implemented laws or regulations that establish the procedures that employers must follow to ensure a fair and reasonable process when dealing with the termination of an employee.

The first step in the process of terminating an employee should be to provide the employee with adequate notice of the dismissal. Depending on the type of dismissal, this can range from a week to a month or more. This notice allows the employee to prepare for the dismissal and make any necessary arrangements. It also gives the employer time to plan how the dismissal will be handled in order to minimize disruption to their business.

The next step is to offer the employee an opportunity to discuss the issues and any potential options to avoid dismissal. The employer should be prepared to explain why dismissal is being considered and ask the employee for any alternatives that can be considered. This is particularly important in cases of disciplinary action, as this provides an opportunity for the employee to explain their actions and potentially avoid dismissal.

The final step in the process should be to document the stages of the process including disciplinary meetings, warnings, and any coaching or training that has taken place. This can help to demonstrate that the process has been fair and reasonable and that the employer has considered all available options before deciding to terminate the employee.

When terminating an employee, employers should also be aware of the various rights to which they are entitled. These rights depend on the jurisdiction and the type of dismissal, but in general, they may include the right to receive a fair wage, the right to receive notice of dismissal, the right to challenge a dismissal, and the right to receive any severance package or other compensation depending on the situation.

As an employer, it is important to ensure that all steps in the process of terminating an employee are fair and reasonable and that the rights of the employee are respected. This includes providing the employee with adequate notice of the dismissal, offering them an opportunity to discuss any potential options to avoid the dismissal, and properly documenting the stages of the process. By following these steps, employers can help to ensure that the process is fair and that the employee is treated with respect.

It is important for employers to ensure that the process is fair and reasonable to avoid any legal ramifications, but more importantly to ensure no collateral damage to the culture. Creating a culture of fear by termination will detract from the growth mindset of an organization. The employee should be made aware of the issues and given an opportunity to discuss the issues and any potential options that may be available to avoid dismissal. Employers should also ensure that the employee is given the opportunity to present their case and make any representations that they may wish to make.

Employers should also ensure that the employee is given adequate notice of the dismissal and any other necessary information including their rights and entitlements. This information should be provided in writing and should include the relevant details of the dismissal process, the date of termination, and any other relevant information such as how to access any termination payments or benefits.

It is important to remember that the decision to dismiss an employee should always be a last resort. Employers should ensure that all reasonable steps have been taken to address the issue and that any coaching or training that is required has been provided. This may include providing additional training or coaching to the employee to help them to improve their performance or to address any disciplinary issues that they may be facing.

The process of dismissal should always be conducted professionally. It should be conducted in private, in a respectful manner, and with consideration for the employee's feelings and rights. Employers should ensure that they use the appropriate language when communicating with the employee and that they are respectful and reasonable in their approach. The employee should be made aware of the reasons for the dismissal and given an opportunity to discuss the issues and any potential options for resolving them.

The dismissal process should also be documented in writing. This documentation should include all relevant details of the process including the date of termination and any other relevant information such as the reasons for the dismissal and any coaching or training that was provided.

Finally, employers should ensure that the employee is supported throughout the process. This may include offering assistance with finding alternative employment or providing career counseling services to help them to find a new job. Employers should also be aware of the potential impact that dismissal can have on the employee's reputation and should ensure that they are not prejudiced by their former employer.

Employers must ensure that they are taking all reasonable steps to ensure that the process of termination is fair and conducted in the best way possible. Terminating an employee can have an enormous impact on both the organization and the individual and employers must consider the rights of the employee and the impact of dismissal on their reputation. The process should be conducted in a professional manner and with consideration for the employee's feelings and rights and should include providing adequate notice of the dismissal and an opportunity to discuss the issues and any potential options to avoid dismissal. Employers should also ensure that they provide the employee with the necessary documentation and support throughout the process

13 TOLERATE – THE FORBIDDEN T

Tolerating poor performance in the workplace is one of the worst ways to handle employees. It creates an environment of lowered expectations and expectations that are not met. When an employee is tolerated and allowed to continue the substandard performance, it sets a precedent that encourages other employees to do the same. This type of environment can have serious implications on the overall productivity and success of the business.

When an employee's poor performance is tolerated, it can have a ripple effect throughout the workplace. This can have a negative impact on morale, productivity, and customer service. Unmotivated employees with poor performance will create an environment of low energy, a lack of motivation, and a lack of enthusiasm. This can lead to a lack of innovation, decreased quality of work, and a lack of team collaboration. Without the motivation and incentive to do a good job, employees may become complacent and not put in the effort they normally would. This can lead to projects taking longer to complete and can lead to missed deadlines and less than stellar customer service.

Tolerating poor performance can also lead to decreased productivity. When an employee's poor performance is tolerated, it sends a message that it is okay to slack off or not do the work that is expected. This can create a culture of mediocrity and can lead to employees not being held accountable. If tasks aren't completed on time or to expected standards, the business will suffer the consequences. Slow productivity can lead to missed deadlines, lost customers, and lower profits.

Furthermore, tolerating poor performance can have a negative impact on customer service. When customers have to deal with employees who lack motivation and enthusiasm, it can cause them to have a negative experience. This can lead to customer complaints and an overall decrease in customer satisfaction. The business will then suffer the consequences of bad reviews and a decrease in sales.

It is important to understand that tolerating poor performance can have serious consequences for a business. Instead of tolerating poor performance, it is important to coach and mentor employees to ensure they are performing to the highest standards. This can help ensure that employees are held accountable, are motivated to do their best, and are producing quality work.

One way to prevent this is to create a culture of accountability. Hold regular meetings to review work, provide feedback, and discuss any areas for improvement. Encourage employees to set goals, create action plans for success, and hold themselves accountable for reaching these goals. This type of culture will help to inspire employees and motivate them to give their best.

It is also important to recognize and reward employees for their achievements. Showing appreciation for their hard work will motivate them to keep up their performance and will help to create an environment of growth and success. Acknowledging the work that employees have done can help them to feel appreciated and will give them the incentive to continue to excel.

It is important to create an environment of open communication. Open communication between managers, supervisors, and employees will help to prevent misunderstandings and miscommunication. It will also help to create a trusting and supportive environment. When employees feel supported and valued, they are more likely to produce high-quality work.

Tolerating poor performance in the workplace is one of the worst ways to handle employees. It can lead to a decrease in morale, productivity, and customer service. Instead of tolerating poor performance, it is important to coach, mentor, and hold employees accountable. By creating a culture of accountability, recognition, and open communication, businesses can ensure their employees are motivated and produce quality work.

Creating a high-accountability environment is essential for any organization or team that desires to achieve success. It is the responsibility of the leader to set the tone for this environment and ensure that everyone is held accountable for their performance. It not only helps to motivate and inspire employees, but also sparks innovation, creativity, and collaboration.

Once expectations have been set, it is important for the leader to regularly monitor performance and provide feedback. This will help to ensure that everyone is meeting their objectives and allow the leader to identify areas for improvement. If performance is not meeting expectations, the leader has to provide coaching and guidance to help get the employee back on track. Leaders have to be held accountable to not ever let Tolerance permeate through a business. It is the kiss of death for a business, morale, and overall performance.

Leaders must hold everyone accountable for their performance. This means setting clear expectations and providing regular feedback on performance. If an employee is not meeting expectations, it is important to provide coaching and guidance in order to get them back on track.

Leaders should also be sure to establish consequences for poor performance. This will help to ensure that everyone is held accountable for their actions and will prevent leaders from tolerating poor performance. Consequences should be tailored to the individual situation and performance issue. Additionally, it is important to be consistent with consequences to ensure fairness and equity.

Leaders should focus on building trust and fostering an atmosphere of open communication, providing clear expectations for employee performance, and rewarding and recognizing individuals for their achievements. Additionally, leaders need to hold everyone accountable for their performance and establish consequences for poor performance in order to prevent leaders from tolerating poor performance. By employing these strategies, leaders can ensure that everyone is held accountable for their actions and create an environment that encourages collaboration and innovation. These strategies are impactful against allowing Tolerance for poor performance.

14 THE PERFORMANCE IMPROVEMENT PLAN

A successful performance improvement plan is an essential part of any business; it helps to ensure that employees are reaching their full potential and performing to the best of their abilities. A performance improvement plan (PIP) is a structured approach to identifying an employee's performance issues, determining the root causes, and developing an action plan to improve performance. The purpose of a PIP is to help employees understand their performance expectations and to provide them with assistance and resources to help them meet those expectations.

The performance improvement plan should be created clearly and concisely, with specific objectives and expectations outlined. It should also include milestones and deadlines to help keep employees on track. Additionally, the plan should be tailored to the individual employee, as every person's goals and skills are different. This document outlines the elements necessary for a successful performance improvement plan.

The first step of a successful performance improvement plan is to set clear and measurable objectives. These objectives should be specific, realistic, and achievable. Furthermore, they should be aligned with the overall organizational goals. This helps ensure that individual employees are contributing to the overall success of the organization.

For example, an objective might include increasing sales by 10% in the next three months. This goal can be broken down into smaller, more measurable goals, such as increasing cold calls by 10% each week or increasing the conversion rate by 5% each month. Additionally, objectives should include a timeline to ensure that progress is being made.

Performance Metrics

The next step of a successful performance improvement plan is to establish performance metrics. Performance metrics are used to measure and evaluate an employee's progress toward their objectives. These metrics should be measurable, actionable, and relevant.

For example, an employee's performance metrics might include the number of sales calls made, the number of sales closed, customer satisfaction rating, and average customer lifetime value. Each of these metrics can be tracked and monitored over time to evaluate an employee's performance.

Resource Allocation

Another important element of a successful performance improvement plan is the allocation of resources. Resources can include anything from time, money, and personnel to technology and equipment.

In order for an employee to reach their objectives, it is important to ensure that they have the tools, materials, and support they need to do their job. For example, a salesperson might need access to a customer relationship management (CRM) system and additional training in order to increase their sales. It is also important to ensure that resources are allocated efficiently and effectively so that they are not wasted.

Feedback

One of the most important elements of a

successful performance improvement plan is feedback. Feedback is essential in order to help employees understand what they are doing well and what they need to improve.

Feedback should be provided on a regular basis and should be both constructive and supportive. Additionally, feedback should be tailored to the individual and should focus on areas where improvement is needed. This helps employees to understand what needs to be done in order to achieve their objectives.

Support

The last element of a successful performance improvement plan is support. It is important that employees feel supported and respected as they work towards their objectives. This can be done through regular communication, recognition, and rewards.

For example, an organization might provide employees with regular feedback, recognition for a job well done, or financial incentives for meeting their goals. Additionally, organizations should provide access to resources, such as mentors or coaching, to help employees reach their objectives.

When it comes to performance improvement plans, there is no one size fits all solution. Each organization is unique, and the strategies that work to address the poor performance of employees in one organization may not necessarily work in another. As a leader, it is important to recognize that each situation requires a tailored solution that takes into account the organization's culture, the individual's personality, and the specific performance issues at hand.

The goal of a performance improvement plan is to help the employee identify and address any areas of deficiency. The plan should also provide the employee with the necessary resources and support to help them improve their performance. It is important to note that the plan should never be used as a punitive measure, but rather as a way to provide the necessary support and resources to help the employee reach their potential.

However, it is natural for employees to feel defensive or resentful when confronted with a performance improvement plan. This is why it is important for leaders to keep in mind that their primary focus should be on helping the employee improve their performance, rather than on punishing them for their mistakes.

Here are some strategies that leaders can use to minimize pushback from poor-performing employees when delivering a performance improvement plan:

1. Prioritize Communication:

Effective communication is essential to any successful performance improvement plan. Leaders should take the time to explain to employees why the plan is necessary and how it will help them improve. It is also important to ensure that employees understand the consequences of not meeting the plan's goals.

When communicating the plan, it is important to emphasize that the focus is on helping the employee improve their performance, not on punishing them. It may also be helpful to provide examples of how the plan has helped other employees in the past.

2. Provide Support and Resources:

In addition to communicating the plan, it is important to provide employees with the support and resources they need to be successful. This may include additional training, mentorship, or access to other resources that can help them reach their goals.

Leaders should also ensure that employees have the necessary time to focus on the plan and that there are adequate resources available to help them meet their goals.

3. Understand the Underlying Issues:

When dealing with a poor-performing employee, it is important for leaders to try and understand the underlying issues that may be causing the performance issues. This could include anything from a lack of motivation or resources to a personal problem that is impacting the employee's ability to succeed.

By understanding the underlying issues, leaders can better tailor the plan to address these issues and help the employee reach their potential.

4. Set Clear Expectations:

When delivering the performance improvement plan, it is important to make sure that employees understand the expectations and goals of the plan. The goals and expectations should be specific, measurable, achievable, relevant, and timely.

Leaders should also make sure that the goals are realistic and that employees have the necessary resources and support to achieve them.

5. Monitor Progress:

It is important to regularly monitor the progress of employees and provide feedback on their performance. This should be done in a constructive and supportive way, and leaders should focus on the areas of improvement rather than on the mistakes.

Leaders should also provide employees with the necessary resources and support to help them reach their goals.

6. Create a Positive Working Environment:

Leaders need to create a positive working environment where employees feel comfortable and supported. This can be done by providing employees with regular feedback, being open and honest about expectations, and recognizing and rewarding employees for their achievements.

Leaders should also ensure that employees have access to the necessary tools and resources to help them achieve their goals.

7. Be Flexible:

Leaders should be open to adjusting the plan as needed to better meet the needs of the organization and the employee. This may include providing additional training, changing the timeline, or allowing the employee to work on alternative projects.

By being flexible and open to adapting the plan, leaders can show employees that they are invested in helping them succeed.

Performance improvement plans should rarely be used as a punitive measure but as an opportunity to help employees improve and reach their potential. When developing and delivering a performance improvement plan, leaders should prioritize communication, provide support and resources, understand the underlying issues, set clear expectations, monitor progress, create a positive working environment, and be flexible. By using these strategies, leaders can minimize pushback from poor-performing employees and help them reach their goals.

15 CREATING A STRATEGY FOR ORGANIZATIONAL IMPROVEMENT

Organizations are complex systems, which require careful consideration, planning, and execution in order to remain competitive and successful. Top management must have a clear vision for how their organization will operate and how it will be structured. In order to improve the efficiency and effectiveness of an organization, a well-crafted strategy must be implemented. This strategy should consider the organization's strengths and weaknesses, as well as its external environment. By understanding and leveraging these elements, an organization can develop an effective strategy to maximize its potential.

The first step in creating a strategy to improve an organization is to assess its current situation.

This involves understanding the organization's current structure, processes, and environment. It is important to take an objective view of the organization and identify areas for improvement. This could include analyzing the organization's goals and objectives, its resources, its customer base, its competitors, and the external environment. By having a comprehensive understanding of the organization's current situation, a strategy can be developed that is tailored to the organization's specific needs.

Once the organization's current situation has been assessed, the next step is to develop a strategy. This should be a well-thought-out plan that outlines the organization's goals and objectives and provides a roadmap for achieving them. The strategy should include both long-term and short-term goals. When developing the strategy, it is important to consider the organization's strengths and weaknesses, as well as its external environment. This will help ensure that the organization is able to leverage its strengths to capitalize on opportunities and mitigate any potential threats.

The strategy should cover all aspects of the organization, from its operations to its marketing, sales, and customer service. This will help ensure that all areas of the organization are working together to support the overall strategy. Additionally, the strategy should be flexible enough to adapt to changing circumstances. This will ensure that the organization can remain competitive and stay ahead of its competitors.

Once the strategy has been created, it is important to communicate it to all members of the organization. This will ensure that everyone understands the organization's vision and is working towards the same goals. This will also help to build a sense of unity and shared purpose within the organization.

In addition to the strategy, it is important to develop a set of metrics to measure the success of the organization. This could include customer satisfaction, sales figures, profitability, and market share. By tracking these metrics, the organization can adjust its strategy as needed in order to achieve its goals.

Finally, it is important to ensure that the strategy is implemented effectively. This requires clear communication and effective leadership. The strategy should be broken down into smaller tasks and assigned to the appropriate individuals. It is also important to provide clear feedback, both positive and negative, to ensure that the strategy is being executed properly.

Creating and implementing an effective strategy is essential for any organization looking to improve. This strategy should be comprehensive and tailor-made to fit the organization's unique needs. By understanding the organization's strengths and weaknesses, and assessing its external environment, an organization can develop a strategy that will help it achieve its goals and remain competitive. Additionally, it is important to communicate the strategy to all members of the organization, develop metrics to measure its success and ensure that it is implemented properly. By following these steps, an organization can improve its efficiency and effectiveness and position itself for long-term success.

Change is an essential element in business and life. While some may view change with trepidation, there are many organizations that welcome and embrace change. Change can bring about new opportunities, solutions to problems, and the ability to grow. While it can be intimidating to strive for change, there are some strategies that can be implemented to ensure success in the process. Creating a reason or crisis to change, implementing accountability, implementing psychological safety, and creating a growth mindset culture are all key components in creating successful change in any organization.

Creating a Reason or Crisis to Change

The initial step in successfully making a change in any organization is creating a reason or crisis to change. This could be a variety of different things, but the most common reasons for seeking change are a decrease in sales, an increase in competition, or a change in customer needs. By identifying the exact reason for the change and communicating it effectively to all stakeholders, leaders can generate buy-in from employees and ensure that everyone is on board with the changes to come.

For example, if a retail store is experiencing a decrease in sales, leaders can use that as a reason to change. They can implement an aggressive marketing strategy, focus on customer service, introduce new products, or even rebrand the store. By identifying the exact reason for the change and communicating it effectively, leaders can create a sense of urgency and inspire the team to take action.

Leaders must also be able to use the change as an opportunity to create a new vision and a new beginning. For example, if a retail store is rebranding, leaders can use this as an opportunity to create a new vision for the store. They can focus on creating a unique customer experience, creating a unique brand identity, and offering exclusive products. By having a clear vision and communicating it to everyone, leaders can create excitement and enthusiasm around the change process.

Implementing Accountability

Once the reason for the change is identified, the next step is to implement accountability. Accountability is essential in any change process as it ensures that everyone is working towards the same goal and that progress is being made. There are several ways to implement accountability in an organization, such as setting clear goals and expectations, having regular check-ins, and providing feedback.

For example, if a retail store is rebranding, leaders should set clear goals and expectations for the project. This could include setting a timeline for completion, deciding on the budget, and outlining the specific tasks that need to be done. By setting clear goals and expectations, leaders can ensure that everyone is on the same page and that progress is being made.

Leaders should also have regular check-ins with

everyone involved in the project. This could be in the form of weekly meetings, individual check-ins, or even group check-ins. This will help to ensure that everyone is on track and that any issues that may arise can be addressed quickly. Finally, leaders should provide feedback throughout the process. This could be in the form of praise, constructive criticism, or even rewards. By providing feedback, leaders can ensure everyone is working towards the same goal and that progress is being made.

Implementing Psychological Safety

In addition to implementing accountability, it is also important to create a culture of psychological safety. Psychological safety is essential in any change process as it allows people to feel comfortable expressing themselves without fear of judgment or repercussions. This can be done in a variety of ways, such as by providing open and honest feedback, creating a nonjudgmental environment, and providing resources for team members to use.

For example, if a retail store is rebranding, leaders should create an environment where feedback is encouraged and appreciated. They should ensure that team members feel safe speaking up and voicing their opinions without fear of judgment or repercussions. Additionally, leaders should make sure to provide resources to team members such as training materials, templates, and other tools that they can use to help them in the rebranding process.

Creating a Growth Mindset Culture

In order to successfully make a change in any organization, leaders must create a culture of a growth mindset. A growth mindset culture is one in which individuals are encouraged to think critically, take risks, and learn from their mistakes.

This can be done in a variety of ways, such as providing access to resources and training, encouraging collaboration, and rewarding creative thinking.

For example, if a retail store is rebranding, leaders should provide access to resources and training that team members can use to help them in the process. This could include access to expert advice, books, podcasts, and other educational materials. Leaders should also encourage collaboration by creating a team environment where team members can brainstorm and discuss ideas. Finally, leaders should reward creative thinking by recognizing and praising team members who come up with innovative ideas or solutions.

Having a growth mindset is essential in leading to success. It's a way of looking at life and challenging oneself to constantly improve and be the best they can be. This mindset focuses on learning from mistakes and failures instead of allowing them to hold someone back and limit their potential. Having environments that promote a growth mindset allows people to reach their goals, develop skills and make an impact in the world around them.

What is a Growth Mindset?

A growth mindset is a belief that a person can improve and develop their skills through hard work, dedication, and effort. It is the belief that they can achieve success and reach their goals by taking on challenges and learning from their mistakes. Those with a growth mindset believe that success lies in their efforts and that failure should be seen as an opportunity to learn and improve. By adopting this kind of outlook, individuals are more likely to stay focused on their goals and cultivate resilience when faced with obstacles.

The idea of a growth mindset was first introduced by world-renowned researcher and psychologist, Dr. Carol Dweck. Dweck's work demonstrates that those with a growth mindset can view failures as learning experiences rather than personal failures. When faced with a difficult situation, they will seek out solutions and see failure as a chance to learn and grow.

In contrast, those with a fixed mindset are more likely to view failure as a personal failure and become discouraged. They may even believe that they're not capable of achieving success. This type of outlook is more likely to lead to a feeling of discouragement and a lack of motivation.

Benefits of a Growth Mindset

The benefits of having a growth mindset are numerous. It allows people to stay focused on their goals and develop resilience. They are also more likely to take on challenges and persist in the face of failure. Having a growth mindset can help individuals become better problem solvers and develop important skills that will serve them well in the future.

Having a growth mindset can also help bolster an individual's self-confidence. People with a growth mindset are more likely to view their efforts positively and focus on the progress they make rather than dwelling on their failures. This can help increase their self-esteem and lead to greater success.

Creating an Environment That Promotes Growth Mindset

Creating an environment that promotes a growth mindset can be beneficial for both individuals and organizations. For individuals, it can help them reach their goals and develop important skills. For organizations, it can help build a culture of learning and development, which can lead to greater success.

There are several steps organizations can take to create an environment that promotes a growth mindset.

1. Celebrate Efforts and Progress

Creating an environment where efforts and progress are celebrated is essential in fostering a growth mindset. It's important to recognize and reward individuals for their hard work and dedication rather than just their successes. This can help create a culture of learning, which can lead to greater success.

2. Foster an Open Environment

Creating an open environment that encourages collaboration and communication is also important. This can help individuals feel comfortable sharing their ideas and suggestions and can encourage creative problem-solving.

3. Encourage Positive Self-Talk

Encouraging positive self-talk is also essential for promoting a growth mindset. This means encouraging individuals to talk positively about themselves, their efforts, and their progress. This can help them develop a more positive outlook and can help them stay focused on their goals.

4. Promote a Learning Culture

Creating a learning culture is also essential for fostering a growth mindset. This means creating an environment where mistakes are seen as learning opportunities rather than failures. It's important to encourage individuals to learn from their mistakes and use them as an opportunity to improve.

5. Promote a Learning Culture

Creating a learning culture is also essential for fostering a growth mindset. This means creating an environment where mistakes are seen as learning opportunities rather than failures. It's important to encourage individuals to learn from their mistakes and use them as an opportunity to improve.

The foundation of an environment built to promote a growth mindset is essential for individuals and organizations alike. It sets the stage for personal development and professional success. The journey towards improvement is a winding, often difficult one, but it's made easier in such an environment. For individuals, it can help them reach their goals and develop important skills such as resilience, grit, creativity, and resourcefulness. For organizations, it can help build a culture of learning and development, which can lead to greater success. It creates an ecosystem where ideas are expressed freely without fear of judgment or retribution, where experimentation is encouraged instead of discouraged. People can share their opinions without the worry of being ostracized with a feeling of safety and support. When the focus is on growth and improvement rather than failure or stagnation, anything is possible.

16 HUMAN LEADERSHIP CAN CHANGE THE WORLD

It is becoming increasingly clear that the health of our people is directly related to the superior-subordinate relationship in the workplace. Harvard Business Review has stated that a person's direct supervisor is more impactful to their health than their primary care. This is a clear indication that the health of our people is largely affected by the attitude of their supervisors and their ability to create an environment conducive to emotional, physical, and mental health.

Employers should prioritize the health and well-being of their people by providing the necessary resources and support to ensure the growth of their workforce. We can do this by instilling a growth mindset among our people, fostering a human-centric leadership approach, and leveraging the power of human capital for meaningful change.

First and foremost, it is important to emphasize the importance of a growth mindset, as this is essential for unlocking the full potential of our people. A growth mindset is an attitude based on the belief that one's abilities and potential can be developed through dedication and hard work. This is a result of understanding that intelligence is not a fixed trait, rather it is something that can be cultivated and improved upon through learning and practice.

Leaders should create an environment that encourages learning and growth by providing the necessary resources and support. This could include investing in employee development and training, as well as offering career development opportunities. It is also important to support employees in their ambitions and encourage them to take risks and pursue their goals. This will ensure that our people are motivated to reach their full potential and develop their skills.

Furthermore, in order to ensure the health and well-being of our people, leaders should prioritize the human-centric approach to leadership. This means taking a more holistic approach to managing people and their health. Leaders should recognize the importance of focusing on the individual and their needs, rather than just on their productivity.

It is important to recognize the positive impact that a strong work-life balance can have on a person's health. This includes allowing employees to take mental health days and providing flexible working arrangements, such as remote working options or shorter working hours. Additionally, employers should be aware of any signs of distress or deterioration in their staff and make sure to provide support and resources.

Employers should also recognize the importance of human capital as an asset. Human capital is the knowledge, skills, and abilities of individuals that can be used to generate value. It is important to invest in the development of our people and to ensure that they have the necessary resources and support to reach their full potential. This could include investing in mentorship programs, providing access to online training and educational resources, and offering coaching and counseling services.

By implementing a growth mindset for our people, a more human-centric leadership approach, and leveraging the power of human capital, we can create a more conducive environment for the health and well-being of our people. This will not only support the success of our organization, but it will ultimately lead to positive changes in the world.

Great leadership can create a world of opportunity and resilience. It can create a place of growth, learning, and ultimately of great success. A leader should strive not only to be successful but also to create an environment where success is infectious, and one in which everyone feels empowered and respected.

One example of great leadership can be seen in the work of Mahatma Gandhi. He had a vision of a world in which everyone could live in peace and harmony, and he was willing to dedicate his life to this cause. He inspired people in India and around the world with his peaceful yet powerful approach to fighting for freedom and justice. He taught people to think for themselves and to take action toward creating a better world. He was an example of how even one person can create change.

Leaders may also be seen in the traditional business world. An effective leader in any field has the responsibility of uniting the team and establishing a shared vision that can be achieved with hard work and dedication. They must be willing to challenge the status quo and strive for excellence, inspiring their team to reach greater heights. This can be seen in the work of many successful business leaders, such as Steve Jobs, Jeff Bezos, and Elon Musk. All of these leaders have inspired change in their respective industries and have set an example for their teams to follow.

Innovation is another key element of great leadership. Good leaders are capable of recognizing new opportunities and leading their teams to explore and capitalize on them. For example, Jack Ma, co-founder of the Chinese e-commerce giant Alibaba, has helped create a platform that has changed the face of commerce worldwide. He has done this by being willing to take risks and by being open to innovation. This has allowed Alibaba to become the largest e-commerce company in the world.

Finally, great leaders must be able to recognize and develop talent. They must be willing to take the time to mentor and support their team and to provide opportunities for their team to grow and learn. For example, Oprah Winfrey has been a successful leader by providing mentorship and support to those in her charge. She has created a platform for people to share their stories, explore their innermost thoughts and feelings, and be open to growth and self-discovery. Through her leadership, she has created an environment where people can explore their potential and reach their goals.

Great leadership can indeed change the world. It can inspire and motivate people to strive for excellence and to challenge the status quo. It can help create a platform for innovation, growth, and success. It can allow people to explore their potential and work together in harmony. By inspiring and supporting their teams, great leaders can create a world of opportunity and resilience.

The hardest questions to answer are;

Will you be brave enough to start the change toward a Growth Mindset?

Will you start to Coach for Growth?

"A journey of a thousand miles begins with a single step"

Chinese Proverb

ABOUT THE AUTHOR

Paul Hylenski is an Aerospace Composites Manufacturing Operations leader who works in Middle River, MD.

Paul started his leadership journey in the Marine Corps. He served as a Helicopter mechanic during his time in the Marines. He served at HMX-1 the Presidential Helicopter Squadron during his time of service.

For the past 15 years, he has worked on multiple different aerospace product lines, managing both the Assembly and Composite fabrication sections of the business. Additionally, he worked as a Six Sigma Blackbelt for the business, focusing on reducing defects and improving output.

Paul is passionate about Leadership because he feels, as leaders, we have the greatest responsibility to be able to make our team's lives better and help them to grow in their careers. He has spent his business career changing culture by implementing psychological safety into aerospace manufacturing.

Paul has written multiple articles about human-centric leadership, has a newsletter on LinkedIn dedicated to the subject, and is the author of the book "Culture Change through Environment Change".

CPSIA information can be obtained
at www.ICGtesting.com
Printed in the USA
LVHW020015280423
745413LV00009B/271

9 781087 890531